THE TEN BEST-KEPT SECRETS
OF TOTAL SUCCESS . . .

are the *only* secrets that separate successful, motivated, "naturally high" people from frustrated, pessimistic ones. Denis Waitley wants you to take control of your life—today! Get in touch with your abilities to love, commit, persevere and win. Use your latent strengths and talents—*you* are the architect of your own totally successful life!

———————

Denis Waitley's extraordinary background includes twenty years of studying the lives of highly successful people. A Naval Academy graduate and former Naval aviator, Dr. Waitley has a Ph.D. in human behavior. He has counseled sales and management executives for Fortune 500 firms, Vietnam POWs and Iranian hostages, as well as Olympic and Super Bowl athletes. He is president of La Jolla Clinic Research Foundation, a visiting scholar to the University of Southern California College of Continuing Education, and is married and the father of six children.

———————

"THIS 20th CENTURY WISE MAN, WHO HAS ALREADY CHANGED SO MANY LIVES FOR THE BETTER THROUGH HIS LECTURES AND HIS WRITINGS, HAS CREATED A MAGIC MIRROR WITH THIS EXTRAORDINARY BOOK THAT WILL REFLECT BACK, TO EACH READER, THE KIND OF PERSON HE OR SHE *CAN* BECOME ONCE THE DORMANT *SEEDS OF GREATNESS* THAT EACH OF US CONTAIN ARE NURTURED AND ALLOWED TO SPROUT AND GROW."

—OG MANDINO, AUTHOR OF
THE GREATEST SALESMAN IN THE WORLD

SEEDS OF GREATNESS

THE TEN BEST-KEPT SECRETS OF TOTAL SUCCESS

DENIS WAITLEY

POCKET BOOKS

New York   London   Toronto   Sydney   Tokyo   Singapore

POCKET BOOKS, a division of Simon & Schuster Inc.
1230 Avenue of the Americas, New York, NY 10020

ISBN 978-1-4516-0755-0

First Pocket Books printing September 1984

26 25 24 23 22 21 20 19 18

POCKET and colophon are registered trademarks of Simon & Schuster Inc.

Printed in the U.S.A.

To my mother, Irene,
who has devoted her life
to caring for others.

And to our children,

Debi, Dayna, Denis, Darren, Kim, and Lisa,
and to "Jake," our first grandchild.

May each of you grow strong and healthy
in your own way,
May you bend and sing with the wind
and reach for the sky . . .
The only ceilings on your growth,
your own imaginations
restless, eager . . .
limitless.

Special Thanks

A word of appreciation to Georglyn Estruth Rosenfeld, who did much of the "spadework" in assembling research material for *Seeds of Greatness*.

Contents

1 | The Seed of Self-Esteem

FROM SELF-LOVE TO SELF-WORTH

2 | The Seed of Creativity

RELEASING YOUR CREATIVE ENERGY

3 | The Seed of Responsibility

WE BECOME WHAT WE DO

4 | The Seed of Wisdom

WHAT IT MEANS TO LIVE "WITHOUT WAX"

5 | The Seed of Purpose

THE GOLD MINE IN YOUR GOALS

6 | The Seed of Communication

REACH OUT AND TOUCH SOMEONE

7 | The Seed of Faith

THE POWER OF POSITIVE BELIEVING

8 | The Seed of Adaptability

TURNING PROBLEMS INTO OPPORTUNITIES

9 | The Seed of Perseverance

THE WILL TO WIN IS EVERYTHING

10 | The Seed of Perspective

TO BE A STAR THROWER

Preface

This is the last self-help book you'll ever need to read. Why do I make such an outlandish claim? Because I believe it. I believe it because I have devoted many years of research in testing the validity of this material. I am a behavioral scientist interested in identifying models for human excellence and wellness. During the past twenty years I have studied astronauts, Olympic and professional athletes, top corporate executives, winning parents and leaders in every field.

Seeds of Greatness reveals ten basic principles of success, supported by the ageless wisdom of the Scriptures and by the latest breakthroughs in medical science. Because these ten principles, while obvious, are so seldom practiced in our society, I call them *The Ten Best-Kept Secrets of Total Success.*

Seeds of Greatness is not a "fad" book; it is a "fact" book—full of truths and values that can endure society's cycles. It contains time-tested attitudes for success which are applicable whether you are a business manager, teacher, computer programmer, engineer, sales executive, trainee, clerk, factory worker, homemaker, parent, athlete or student.

It is for you if you have never really succeeded; if you just want more of the same success you now enjoy; or if you have made it, lost it, and would like to get it again, and keep it!

The work is unique in that it explains complex psychological concepts in easy-to-understand language, using real life examples for maximum reader interest and comprehension. It explains and documents the attitudes exemplified by high-performance, happy individuals in their professional and personal lives. It also shows the reader how to change his or her own daily life-style for the better, using proven behavior modification techniques and self-management methods.

This is a book to read, reread, study, underline, discuss, and pass along to employees, friends, and family members. Instead of a "one-shot, quick fix" to humor you or make you feel better for a day or two, it is a do-it-yourself daily lifeguide. The ten chapters offer solutions for some of the most pressing problems that confront each of us.

The following are questions that inspired the research in this book:

- What kind of individuals are the happiest and most productive?
- What are the rare characteristics of leadership in a manager or parent?
- How can we gain control of our thoughts, our reactions, and our time?
- How can we become emotionally well, physically fit, and spiritually sound?

As you begin to read, you should ask yourself a few other questions so that you can benefit most from the material:

- Would employees like to have me for a boss?
- Would I like to have me for a spouse?
- Would team members like to have me for a coach?
- Would I like to have me for a parent?
- Would I like to have me for a friend?

You may answer "Yes" to some of the above and "I'm not sure" to others. Whatever your answers, this book will have special significance to you. I believe you are going to love this book. I believe it will change the way you look at life—starting today!

Prologue

Grandma Taught Me to Plant the Seeds

Oh, how beautiful she was—and is—to me. When the Christmas tree lights are first plugged in; when we say grace at the Thanksgiving table; whenever I see a hummingbird whirring motionless at our hanging nectar feeder; when I walk in our rose garden shortly after dawn among the exquisite crimson, white, pink, and yellow buds and smell their fragrance; when I think of natural treasures . . . I think of hand trowels . . . I think of kneeling in the freshly turned earth, and planting seeds with her . . . my grandmother.

I've flown in a Navy jet nearly twice the speed of sound, landed on aircraft carriers, played my share of contact sports, and always considered myself a "macho" man (although I do enjoy seafood quiche and walks on the beach) . . . but there is something about my memories of my grandma, Mabel, that makes my eyes mist over. She was fifty-three when I was nine. That's when we planted our first "Victory" garden together, in 1942, about six months after the outbreak of World War II. My grandma and I shared one of those special relationships as rare as a double rainbow. We planted seeds together—in the soil—and in each other.

Her effect on my value system has been matched by only one other person I have encountered in all of my

19

life—my precious wife, Susan. My grandma lived eighty-seven seasons without a complaint. I was forty-three when I last saw her. But I remember every mince tart, every bite of "made from scratch" apple pie, and each lingering wave of her hand as she stood (out of sight, or so she thought) by the rayon, priscilla curtains in her little house at 718 West Pennsylvania Avenue in San Diego. Our station wagon full of kids and contentment would slowly pull away from the curb—we would all look back at her and wave—and I would gaze at her fragile silhouette through the rear view mirror, wishing I could frame her there forever—just that way—wondering how many more Christmas dinners we would share.

Most of all, I remember my grandma and me planting seeds. We planted squash, beans, corn, watermelons, beets, pansies, mums, and other flowers. I'll admit I rode my bike those twenty miles each Saturday more for the bonus of the conversation and the homemade pastries, than for the vegetables and flowers. But no matter how full I was after all I ate, I was always left hungry for more of what she told me about her past and my future. I felt like "Dickon" in Frances Hodgson Burnett's classic book, *The Secret Garden,* when I pedaled off on the two-hour journey to my grandma's home. I could hardly wait until I got there, and I never wanted to leave.

She told me about her life in England before she arrived in America, seasick and awestruck. I was dumbfounded to learn that she and her sister had to carry their candles way out in front of them in a certain position, as they went up the stairway each night to their room, so that they wouldn't set their bedclothes on fire. I couldn't believe it when she recounted her list of daily chores, including taking the meat, cheese, and milk down to the cellar and putting them on the large stone to keep them cool and fresh as possible for another day or two. They didn't even have iceboxes then, or icemen with a block of ice in a sack on their backs, with tongs to deliver it once or twice a week! She smiled, when I complained about how bad things were in her childhood, and she said that "things don't matter as much as your attitude toward them." I didn't understand exactly what she meant by that when I was nine, but after a few more years in our "Secret Garden," her wisdom began to take root in me.

In June of 1946, when I had just turned thirteen, she mentioned something in passing that has had a profound effect on my professional and personal life. She had successfully crossed an apricot tree with a plum tree years before and it was finally bearing fruit. Our excitement on that occasion was something like I witnessed in my youngest children when they saw the movie *E.T.* for the first time. "What do you suppose this fruit will taste like?" she teased, holding the stepladder firm so that I could reach the ripest pink balls hanging in the upper branches. "Gee, I can't imagine how they'll taste, Grandma," I replied. "Do you suppose they'll be any good?" "Why of course they will be delicious," she chided. "Didn't we do the planting, nurturing, and the pruning?"

Sure enough, they were delicious, even though they looked unlike any plums or apricots I'd ever seen before. "That's because they are uniquely unlike any other fruit you'll ever eat," she said, as I attempted to wipe the juice off the front of the new shirt she had given me for my birthday the week before. "They are plumcots!" she exulted. "You always get out what you put in," she continued as we sat under the tree eating most of what we had picked. "Plant apple seeds and you get apple trees, plant acorns and you get great oak trees, plant weeds and you will harvest weeds, plant the seeds of great ideas, and you will get great individuals," she said softly and intently, looking directly into my eyes. "Do you understand what I mean?" I nodded, remembering that I'd heard her say the same thing before, in different ways.

We went into the house, so that she could wash my

shirt and hang it out to dry before I rode my bike on the two-hour return trip back home, before dark, with a bag of plumcots for my brother and sister.

As she was ironing my shirt, I listened, enthralled, as she completed the analogy between seeds of great ideas and the growth of great individual lives. She had worked for forty years as a proofreader for a local book printer and I marveled at her command of words. Here was my grandma, with no formal schooling beyond junior high, married with three children by the time she was nineteen, who lived alone and cared for herself for thirty-eight years after my grandfather died in his forties of double-pneumonia. She was the guiding force for her seven grandchildren, expressing a depth of human insight and psychological brilliance that I have not heard again, even after twenty years of the finest education scholarships can buy, and after twenty additional years of meeting and working with some of the most respected medical and behavioral scientists in the United States.

"The Seeds of Greatness," she began, "what are they? Are they special genes, transmitted to offspring by superior parents? Are they in-born talents? Are they seeds of exceptional learning abilities or intelligence quotients (IQs)?" "No," my grandma shook her head emphatically, "the Seeds of Greatness are not dependent upon the gifted birth, the inherited bank account, the intellect, the skin-deep beauty, the race, the color or the status. The Seeds of Greatness are attitudes and beliefs that begin in children as baby talk, as do's and don'ts, as casual family chatter, bedtime stories, locker-room gossip—as offhanded, almost unnoticed, delicately transparent ideas, like flimsy cobwebs, at first—then, with years of practice, become like unbreakable steel cables to shackle or strengthen our characters throughout the rest of our adult lives."

I asked my grandma what I should do to plant great ideas in myself, so that I could have a great life. She told me to follow the lessons of the Bible and model my thoughts and actions after men and women who have been creative in their service to others. She advised me to look at my IQ as my *"Imagination* Quotient," rather than my Intelligence Quotient. I learned that Jules Verne in the nineteenth century not only placed in Florida the site of the spaceport for the first manned expedition to the moon, but that he also described his imaginary moon shot in remarkable detail. When I was twenty years older, my grandma and I saw the 1969 Apollo 11 trip closely resemble the Jules Verne version. I heard about the Halloween-eve radio broadcast, when I was five, by a young announcer named Orson Welles, who warned Americans that "the War of the Worlds" was really beginning, and that giant robots had landed in New Jersey. My grandma said that there were heart attacks, strokes, and suicides and that many people panicked, packing their belongings and crowding the roads—imagining that the robots would crush them too! When she told me those true stories, I began to understand how people succeed or fail in their imagined experiences. She stroked my forehead, kissed me and sent me on my way—more than thirty years ago.

Today, as we approach the end of the twentieth century, I sit in my study loaded with Atari cartridges, enough Apple software to manage NASA, and biofeedback instruments to help me control my autonomic body functions. But my thoughts are there, beneath the plumcot tree with my hand trowel, and that lovely lady with whom I planted early seeds. Could it have been thirty years ago? Now I know what people mean when they say, "It seems like only yesterday."

The Meaning of Total Success

"Model your thoughts and actions after men and women who have been creative in their service to others," my grandmother had counseled. Armed with that affirmation, I ventured forth like the hero in "Jack and the Beanstalk," with a handful of "magic seeds," reaching out and up in search of the goose that laid the golden egg. Ever since my curiosity was aroused, nearly forty years ago, about the pursuit of excellence as a human being, I have devoted much of my life to learning from the examples of people for whom I have worked and with whom I have developed a personal as well as professional relationship.

In addition to my grandmother and my mother who almost always provided positive nurturing in my growth process, there are several individuals who stand out among all the others, who have taught me some definitions and secrets of successful living. Abraham Maslow, with his hierarchy of needs; Maxwell Maltz, who, through the plastic surgeon's magic wand, was able to explain in understandable terms the cybernetic nature of the self-image; and Hans Selye, the early pioneer of stress research—I learned a secret from my personal encounter with each of them. Although their work here upon the earth has been completed, what they have planted are but seedlings offering abundance for future generations.

My work at the Salk Institute for Biological Studies near my hometown in La Jolla, California, brought me in close contact with Dr. Jonas Salk, who developed the first and most effective vaccine against polio. By reading his books, observing his work, and having some rare private moments to chat, I gained confidence that I should concentrate on studying "life and health" rather than "disease and cure." Jonas Salk, in his wisdom and scientific evidence, has taught me the real meaning of cooperation and order in the universe. Norman Vincent Peale, Carl Rogers, Robert Schuller, Viktor Frankl, Ken Cooper, Art Linkletter, Og Mandino, Wilma Rudolph, John Haggai, Robert Anderson, Lloyd Conant, and Archie McGill—each of these individuals has touched my life with special insight into the potential for human fulfillment.

But no better definition of success has been penned

by anyone than that offered by Earl Nightingale—whom I consider to be one of the greatest philosophers of our time—in his classic recording, "The Strangest Secret" (which, incidentally, is the only narrative, nonmusical recording ever to sell over a million copies). Earl's definition is: *"Success is the progressive realization of a worthy ideal."* It means that when we are working or moving toward something we want to accomplish, especially when that something brings us respect and dignity as members of the human race, we are succeeding. It has nothing to do with talent, IQ, education, age, race, birth, money, or power. It doesn't mean "getting there," "being there," "having it all," "fame and fortune," "looking down from the summit," or "being with the in-crowd."

Success in the United States is usually associated with material wealth. The image of shaded estates with electric gates, a Rolls or Ferrari in the circular driveway, Gucci accessories, private jets, yachts, Greek Islands, and luxurious leisure bombards our senses. The only problem is that Ricardo Montalban never greets us at the airport in his white tuxedo, with "Tattoo," to complete our fantasy. Ninety percent of us simply aren't going to live in that kind of setting. And if we think that represents success, then we're not going to be successful during our lives. There is no question that money is the source of power for good and evil, that resource is behind all research, that farmland must be financed in order to provide food. But that's the point. It is not what you *get* that makes you successful, it is *what you are continuing to do with what you've got*.

About 95 percent of the human beings on earth are poor, the majority of them desperately poor. Success to any member of such a family is to have some land to till, any job that pays, and a way to earn enough to provide nourishment for the children to grow in decent health into adulthood. Financial wealth is the harvest of our productivity. It can be used to boost the productivity of others. It is important, and with it we can live and enjoy the good life. I believe in enjoying the fruits of my labors without guilt. I also believe in the Double Win—if I help you with your needs, then I win too!

Among leaders in every field there is an amazing convergence of opinion on what is "total success" in life. The consensus is that the two great tragedies are "never to have had a dream to strive for" and "ever to have fully reached it." Happiness seems to be associated more with the experience of the journey, than in the fleeting moment of the recognition of having arrived. Although no one ever will achieve "total success" in his or her daily pursuits, a definition of success you can live by is this:

Total success is the continuing involvement in the pursuit of a worthy ideal, which is being realized for the benefit of others—rather than at their expense.

Grandma would have liked that definition. It epitomizes her philosophy of life and success, and no one was a greater success than my grandmother.

Success is the process of learning, sharing, and growing. When I think of success, I think of the word *commencement*. Is a high school commencement ceremony really the completion of high school, or graduation to a new beginning in college or career? It is both. Every completion has a new beginning. We need to seed and cultivate our gardens. The need to work in the garden never ends; it is never finished, never done.

SEEDS OF
GREATNESS

1 | The Seed of Self-Esteem

My friends Stan and Georglyn own a Yorkshire Terrier. He's a cute little fellow, with beautiful long hair that needs to be brushed every day. Actually, "Buckwheat" doesn't really belong to my friends; he belongs to their daughter Natalie.

When Natalie and her parents moved into a new home in Mesa, Arizona, they put in a swimming pool to take advantage of the climate. They planted what was to be a lush, green lawn around the pool and installed underground sprinklers. Buckwheat couldn't keep his nose out of anything. He kept falling into the pool and would either climb out or have to be fished out. Then he would shake furiously to dry off and then roll in the fertilizer on top of the new lawn. When Natalie tried to brush his matted hair, he would yelp and snap at her.

What "Buckwheat" Taught Us about Self-Esteem

Every day Buckwheat explored his new domain. Whenever the sprinklers would pop up automatically, catching him off guard, he would chase and bite the spray from these "invaders," barking incessantly to warn the family. When Natalie's brother, Nathan, backwashed the pool, the long hose thrashed back and forth like a fire hose with no one holding on. Buckwheat came to the rescue and charged valiantly into the water, growling and biting the enemy.

After the battle he would roll in the fertilizer again, which looked like the center of a football field in the fourth quarter, on a rainy day. Buckwheat looked like he had played center on the losing team! His mud-tangled coat was beyond repair. Later, at the dog grooming clinic, the prognosis was what the family had feared—Buckwheat's hair was terminal! It took three people to hold him down during the operation, which consisted of shaving him almost to the skin.

The reception back home was not what little Buckwheat had expected, after all he'd been subjected to. When he was carried in the door, the other kids—Leah and Halie—laughed and made fun of him because he didn't look like a beautiful "Yorkie" any more. He looked more like a giant rat from a science fiction movie in which nature gets revenge on technology, with a strange mutation.

Buckwheat reacted to the teasing by hiding under the living room sofa. Instead of jumping into everyone's lap, licking every available face, he cowered out of sight. When he finally found it necessary to get food or water, he sneaked behind the couch and chairs to his dish after the family had left the kitchen area. He sat in a corner of the house for two days, shivering uncontrollably when anyone would come near him. It took several days of constant loving, holding, and stroking by the family before he was convinced that he was still accepted.

I tell this story because it taught all of us a crucial lesson. When Buckwheat lost his beautiful coat he lost more than beauty. The derisive laughter told him that he no longer belonged. His shivering was not caused primarily by the cold; he felt afraid, alone, and rejected. In short, Buckwheat's self-esteem plunged to zero. His fearful trembling was not that much different from the cowering of thousands of human beings who are hiding in the shadows of rejection. And Buckwheat's recovery of good self-esteem—accomplished only with much stroking and caring—illustrates perfectly the most precious gift that can be given or received: the gift of love.

The First Best-Kept Secret of Total Success

There are many definitions and interpretations of love. I've always looked at love as unconditional acceptance and "looking for the good." Perhaps one of the best and most appropriate descriptions of love is that given by Dr. Gerald Jampolsky, a well-known psychiatrist, author and founder of the Center for Attitudinal Healing in Tiburon, California. Dr. Jampolsky teaches children and adults experiencing emotional and physical crises that "love is letting go of fear."

With love, there can be no fear. Love is natural and unconditional. Love asks no questions—neither preaching nor demanding; neither comparing nor measuring. Love is—pure and simple—the greatest value of all.

> **The First Best-Kept Secret of Total Success is that we must feel love inside ourselves before we can give it to others.**

Simple, isn't it? If there is no deep, internalized feeling of value inside of us, then we have nothing to give to or share with others. We can need them, we can be dependent upon them, we can look for security in them, we can indulge them, flatter them and attempt to purchase them. But we cannot share or give an emotion to anyone else, unless we first possess that emotion inside of us.

Don't Be Fooled by the Mask I Wear

Since I am treating *Seeds of Greatness* as my personal letter to you, I'd like to share with you portions of a letter I discovered during the research on this book. The author is unknown to me, but the words could easily have been written by some inner voice that hides, unseen, in each of us, whispering of our fragile sensitivity and vulnerability to our imagined fears of rejection.

Don't be fooled by me. Don't be fooled by the face I wear. I wear a mask. I wear a thousand masks—masks that I am afraid to take off; and none of them are me.

Pretending is an art that is second nature to me, but don't be fooled. For my sake, don't be fooled. I give the impression that I am secure, that all is sunny and unruffled within me as well as without; that confidence is my name and coolness my game, that the water is calm and I am in command; and that I need no one. But don't believe me, please. My surface may seem smooth, but my surface is my mask, my ever varying and ever concealing mask.

Beneath lies no smugness, no complacence. Beneath dwells the real me in confusion, in fear, in aloneness. But I hide that. I don't want anybody to know it. I panic at the thought of my weakness and fear being exposed. That's why I frantically create a mask to hide behind—a nonchalant, sophisticated facade—to help me pretend, to shield me from the glance that knows. But such a glance is precisely my salvation, my only salvation, and I know it. That is, if it's followed by acceptance; if it's followed by love.

It's the only thing that can liberate me from myself, from my own self-built prison wall, from the barriers I so painstakingly erect. It's the only thing that will assure me of what I can't assure myself—that I am really something. . . .

Who am I, you may wonder. I am someone you know very well. I am every man you meet. I am every woman you meet. I am every child you meet. I am right in front of you. Please . . . love me.[1]

If fear of rejection prevents us from being loved and from expressing love, how do we let go of it? What do we tell the subconscious voice inside of us that controls our "feelings" toward ourselves and others?

Fear: *False Education Appearing Real*

I believe the way to conquer fear is to understand its roots, then soften the earth around it with new enlight-

---

1. Dov, Pereta, Elkins, *Glad to Be Me* (New York: Prentice-Hall, 1976), pp. 28, 29.

enment, then pull it out—planting the seed of love where fear stood tall. I look at fear as *F*alse *E*ducation *A*ppearing *R*eal. In my experience, there are three dominant fears, beyond the fear of death, which is the greatest fear among nonspiritual individuals:

> Fear of Rejection, which is being made a fool or failure in the sight or presence of others.
> Fear of Change, which is charting unknown waters, being first, breaking tradition, sacrificing external security.
> Fear of Success, which is an expression of guilt associated with our natural desire for self-gratification.

The Fear of Rejection begins early in childhood as we encounter the first "No!" in our natural exercise of curiosity to explore and gratify our own needs. Even before a child is born, the nurturing moods of its mother during the nine-month pregnancy are important, as are the environmental noise levels and the substances the mother consumes, as a reflection of her own self-worth.

Toddlers need to receive encouragement as they attempt to master early skills; they need praise when they succeed, and understanding when they fail. If raised in a nurturing family environment, toddlers also experience two other most important steps in their healthy development toward adulthood. They develop their first meaningful, loving relationship with another person, usually the parent of the opposite sex, which is natural; and they establish ownership of objects and special places all their own. This building of identity—of possessing value—is an important ingredient in the quality of self-esteem.

Teenagers need to establish independence, discover new relationships and competency outside of the family; they need acceptance as they are, rather than for their achievements according to materialistic standards; and they need praise.

It's amazing how parents continue to pass their own hang-ups on to their children. It reminds me of the story about the young bride who cooked a ham for her new husband. Before putting it in the pan, she cut off both ends. When her husband asked her why she did that, she replied that her mother had always done it that way. At a later date, when they were having baked ham dinner at her mother's home, he asked her, casually, why she cut both ends off the ham. The mother shrugged and said she really didn't know, except that her mother had always done it that way. Finally, he asked the grandmother why she always cut the ends off the ham before she baked it. She looked at him suspiciously, replying, "Because my baking dish is too small!"

How the Weeds of Fear Are Planted

This is not a book on effective parenting, per se, although I believe it can help. It is intended to be on general leadership. Since fear is such a universal negative motivator that either compels or inhibits everywhere it appears, it's important for us to realize that many of our fears do stem from childhood as a direct result of threatened value.

The Fear of Rejection can be traced to early criticisms we received from our parents, other members of our families, in some cases our teachers, and most definitely our peers. It is the association of ourselves with our mistakes. Parents make the classic mistakes in raising their children by saying "Bad Boy" or "Naughty Girl," "Shape Up or Ship Out," and in effect, "If you're not good the Baby Buyer's coming by, and we won't ask much for *you*." "Crybaby." "Whiner Puss." "Spoiled Brat." "Loud Mouth." "Clumsy."

While we parents really mean for these labels to apply to our children's behavior, unfortunately the child takes them personally, unable to separate who he or she *is*, from what he or she *does*. That's called confusing the doer with the deed. It's devastating to a child.

As children become of school age they get it from parents and peers, coming and going. "Fatso," "Beaver Teeth," "Buzzard Beak," "Freckle Face," "Bean Pole," "Ugly," "Dumbo Ears," "Four Eyes," "Stupid," "Motor Mouth," "Metal Mouth," "Sloppy," "Lazy," "Hulk," "Old Unreliable," "Punker," "Gross," "Uncoordinated," and so forth.

When we're in college or professional life, it's not much different. "Radical," "Dense," "Boring," "Square," "Straight," "Weird," "Bigot," "Establishment," "Uptight," "Wild," "Uninteresting," "Klutz," "Loser."

Children who grow up in environments full of "putdowns," negative "nicknames," and criticism often become critical adults, with less than adequate self-esteem. The Fear of Rejection becomes The Fear of Change, and they tend to seek security and positions where you go with the system and don't "rock the boat." The Fear of Change translates into The Fear of Success. And The Fear of Success, in my opinion, is almost as strong as The Fear of Rejection.

The reason The Fear of Success is so prevalent in our society is the manner in which we are trained as children. First, we are cuddled as infants. Then, we start to learn that there are a lot of things we're not good at, and there are a lot of things we're not supposed to do, and, more importantly, we observe our role models on TV putting each other down, fighting and killing each other, ruining each other's lives, and then, miraculously, making up at the end of the hour. We observe our role models at home—our parents—preoccupied with their financial problems, sometimes not very loving to each other, and shaking their heads in disgust when they watch the evening news as "the window on our wonderful world." Before we are sent out into this world as teenagers or young adults (kids are staying longer at the "Hometel" these days), we are given instructions that it's a lot worse today than when our parents ventured forth. We're warned that because of inflation we'll never be able to afford a nice home on a fairly nice lot and that instead we can look forward to a condo twelve stories high, on one-sixth of an acre, with a freeway view.

While all these put-downs are going on, the strangest paradox is occurring. Our parents, feeling guilty that they have spent so little time enjoying our youth with us, attempt to purchase our love by indulging us with money—unearned—and possessions they never could afford for themselves. And, finally, they tell us to go out and Win, fight for our rights, do better than they did, and they remind us in subtle ways, "After all we sacrificed a lot to invest in your future, so don't blow it!"

The result is The Fear of Success syndrome, which is really the fear of trying. Its manifestations are rationalization and procrastination. "I can't imagine myself successful." "I can see it for you, but I can't see it for me." "I went down to apply at 8:30, when they said to be there, but the line was halfway down the block, so I left." "I would like to, but I don't have enough experience." "I'm going to look into that, when I have more time . . . after I retire."

Most individuals realize that common people have become uncommonly productive by using their creative imaginations. They have observed the biographies of individuals who have overcome enormous handicaps and roadblocks to become great. But they can't imagine it happening to themselves. They resign themselves to mediocrity and even failure, wishing and envying away their lives. They develop the habit of looking back at past problems (failure reinforcement); and imagining similar performances in the future (failure forecasting). Because they are controlled by rejection and acceptance standards set by others, they often set their sights unrealistically high. Not really believing in the validity of their dreams, and not preparing enough for their achievement, they fall short again and again.

Failure becomes set in their self-images. Just when they seem to break through, get on top, or make real progress—they blow it! In truth, The Fear of Success caused them to procrastinate the preparation and creative action necessary for success. And rationalization sets in to satisfy the subconscious feeling that "you can't expect to get ahead, when you've been through what I have."

How to Lead (and Love) without Fear

How do we redirect our thinking and help others overcome the three great fears? Here are some practical rules to follow in the leadership of employees or children:

1. *Separate Performance from Performer*

   In communicating with others, always treat *behavior* and *performance* as being *distinctly separate* from the *personhood* or *character* of the individual you are trying to influence.

   Bad: "You're a liar!"
   Better: "That statement doesn't match my inputs; let's check it out together."
   Bad: "Your supervisor reports that you're lazy and unproductive."
   Better: "Your supervisor and I believe that you're capable of a higher level of output. If I can be of any help, that's my job."
   Bad: "Clean up your room, you pigs!"
   Better: "All of the bedrooms in our home

are neat and clean. While you're cleaning up the room, I'll be at the store. When I get back, I'll show you a way to help separate your clothes better, in the closet."

Bad: "You'll never make college, unless you shape up. With this report card, you'll be lucky to find a job in a video arcade."

Better: "Although I didn't say much when I looked at your report card, I know you can do better than that report shows. I went up to school and talked to your counselor and some of your teachers, and they're confident that you can make a real contribution to the class. I believe you will. I love you and I know you'll always do your best, and that's what counts. I'm really interested in your life. Is there anything I can do to help you more?" (This last long answer is an actual response to a below average report card from one of my own children. As a result of our showing an interest in the child and separating the *performance* (grades) from the *performer* (child), the grades improved dramatically; with constant reinforcement, the child made the honor roll and continues to expect good results—not perfection— just good results.)

2. *Criticize the Performance, Praise the Performer*

Whenever performance reprimands are

given, a *positive stroke to the individual should follow immediately* on the heels of the reprimand.

Bad: "You're late on almost every production schedule, and if you continue the same pattern, the department is going to lose money this year."

Better: "I need your help in meeting our production deadlines. The department needs increased efficiency to be profitable, and I expect more direct influence from you. *Incidentally, I'm getting good feedback from the field on quality and performance from you. Thanks to you we have fewer customer complaints.*"

Bad: "If you don't stop drinking so much at the Club every weekend, I'm going to start going somewhere else by myself."

Better: "How about breaking our routine next weekend and going to that road-show version of the Broadway show we've been talking about. I called and tickets for Saturday night are available. *I'd like to start spending more quality time, just with you.*"

Bad: "I can't complain about your defensive play, but you've got to concentrate more and stop missing those free throws from the foul line. Missing free throws is what loses big games."

Better: "Teams with high free-throw percentages win ball games. Since they are free points, let's make all we can. Put in an extra fifteen minutes a day on practicing your free throws next week. *Boy, your defensive play looks sharp.*"

3. *Always reprimand performance in private. Praise in private, also, if the praise is intended to single someone out of a group.* Public disapproval is the worst form of punishment, and leads to low self-esteem, as well as fear of rejection and fear of success. Public praise creates peer jealousy among employees and sibling rivalry among family members, especially if there are spoken or unspoken comparisons that can be made. The most powerful forms of praise are one-on-one, in private, when the recipient least expects them; and at a special award ceremony that has been anticipated by all concerned.

So, then, the gift of value is the absence of fear. People who live with fear grow up standing at the end of every line. People who live with praise learn to stand alone and lead their parade, even if it's raining. People who are spoiled with indulgence and permissiveness grow up full of compromise and greed. People who are given challenges and responsibilities grow up with values and goals. People who live with depression will need a drink, a puff, a pill to get them high. People who live with optimism will grow up thinking they were born to fly!

People who live with hate grow up blind to beauty and true love. People who live with love live to give their love away and are blind to hate. If our people are reminded of all the bad we see in them, they'll become exactly what we hoped they'd never be! But if we tell our people, "We're so glad you're in the game," they'll be glad to be alive, right now, and glad they wear their name!

How to Hang On to Your Dreams

Successful people believe in their own worth, even when they have nothing but a dream to hang on to. Why? Because their own self-worth is stronger than the rejection or acceptance of their ideas by others.

As I mentioned in the Prologue, success is a "commencement" in life. Every completion means a new beginning. Material achievements are standards of excellence in products or projects that fill a need. There is just as much value in the inventor *before* his product is mass-produced as there is after he has made his fortune. And in so knowing, he or she has the courage to go forward.

Elias Howe invented the sewing machine and the women laughed for years. With their sewing done so quickly, they argued, what in the world would they find to do with all that extra time? He lived his life in borrowed suits, yet his machine has done more than any other to create the clothes he could never afford to buy.

One man, a college professor, was both intelligent and inquisitive. His sister had a hearing deficiency and in trying to invent a device to enhance her hearing, he created something more complex. After many years of trial and error and success, he was ready to take it into production. More years were spent traveling throughout New England trying to get venture capital interest in his dream. They laughed when he suggested that he could carry the human voice along a wire so that it could be heard for miles. Indeed! They laughed that he would have the nerve to assume it would work for even one mile. Nobody laughs at Bell today. Alexander Graham Bell had the self-esteem to hang in there when the only reward was his belief in himself.

Walt Disney was said to have asked ten people what they thought of a new idea and if they were unanimous in their rejection of it, he would begin work on it immediately. Of course, he was used to being rejected. He was bankrupt when he went around Hollywood with his little "Steamboat Willie" cartoon idea. Can you imagine him trying to sell a talking mouse, with a falsetto, in silent movie days? Walt dreamed the big dream, and children everywhere, from Disney World in Japan to Epcot Center in Florida, will be forever grateful. Was Walt Disney a better man while he was broke and still narrating the original voice of Mickey Mouse, or after he made all those great movies . . . or after he built Disneyland . . . or after he built Walt Disney World in Orlando? Value is in the doer, not the deed.

Every time I think of Golda Meir, I say how dare she be that brilliant to presume that a common woman could be the prime minister of a major country? She was plain, but beautiful inside. And how could Margaret Thatcher, living over her father's grocery store until she was twenty-one—how dare she think enough of herself to lead England in these troubled times? What a late bloomer Grandma Moses was! She didn't start painting until she was in her seventies and painted over 500 celebrated works of art. And nobody liked Renoir's work. One Parisian expert looked over his paintings and sneered: "You are, I presume, dabbling in paint to amuse yourself." And Renoir replied: "Of course, when it ceases to amuse me, I will stop painting."

Earl Nightingale, in his radio program "Our Changing World," tells the story of Renoir, as if history were alive. He says that everyone told Renoir to give up painting, because he had no talent. A group of artists who were rejected by the establishment of their time formed their own little group consisting of Degas, Pissarro, Monet, Cézanne, and Renoir—five of the all-time great masters, doing what they believed in, while the others laughed. Earl goes on to say that in Renoir's later life he suffered from advanced rheumatism, particularly in his hands. When Matisse stopped by to see the aging painter, he noticed that every brush stroke was causing Renoir great pain. And Matisse asked: "Why is it that you still have to work? Why do you continue to torture yourself?" And Renoir slowly answered: "The pain passes, but the pleasure, the creation of beauty, remains."

You Are a Masterpiece of Creation

I may never be an artist like Renoir, but I've painted interiors and exteriors of several of our houses through the years that I'm proud of. You and I may not be the king or queen of a royal court, but we are special in our own right. Wouldn't it be wonderful if all the children in the world felt they were unique and special just because they were alive? If we can overcome poverty and disease, the next step will be to teach people that the most important "labels" in society are the ones we hang on ourselves.

I've always observed that leadership is the only profession for which there is no formal training or education. It seems that if you want to learn about something, it's best to try teaching it to someone else. No one ever learns as much as the teacher. In addition to going to school on my own mistakes as a father in trying to raise six physically and emotionally healthy children, I also lead seminars for preteens, teens, young adults, and corporate executives. At the beginning of the preteen self-esteem workshop, we bring eight volunteers to the front of the class and give them a project. Each of the eight is given a cardboard "status" sign to hang around his or her neck to show off what his or her particular status is in life. A title is printed in big letters on the front of each sign: Baby, Mother, Astronaut, Janitor, Rock Star, NBA Basketball Player, Doctor, and Lawyer. The assignment is for the children to position themselves in the order of their importance in front of the rest of the group. The age range is 7 to 11.

What starts out as a harmless exercise turns into *Star Wars* and *Virginia Woolf*. After the pushing and shoving stops and they settle down to serious "status seeking," they finally begin to form a kind of hierarchical line, according to a consensus pecking order. Up walks the Astronaut to the front of the line. "I'm first, because I'm going places where the rest of you can't go yet. And, besides, I'm going to try to find us another place to live, 'cause earth is too crowded." (Applause from spectators.)

Up walks the Rock Star, and pushes the Astronaut to second place. (Cheers from spectators.) "I'm already in Outer Space, and I make the most money, and could buy you as the pilot for my private jet."

Next comes the NBA Basketball Player. "I think I should go first. I make just as much money as the Rock Star and I play to a big crowd every night, all season, doing something physical, which is better for you." (More cheers.)

Up walks the Doctor to make his run at first place. "I should go first because I fix all of you when you're injured or sick, and I make good money too." (Light applause.)

Up walks the Lawyer. "I'm the best, because I put you in jail or keep you out of jail, and you have to pay me all your money." (Cheers).

Up walks the Mother. "I really am first, because I brought all of you into the world." (Light applause.)

Up walks the Baby to the front. "Shouldn't I really be the first in line because all of us were babies, before we were mothers, or anything else?" (Applause.)

That still leaves the Janitor. Well, as usual, he or she knows better than to try to go up front. Those who play the Janitor role either don't try, knowing they'll be laughed at. Or they start to say something, and are laughed at, or poked fun at so much, that they are too embarrassed to continue even though it is a game in which all participants are volunteers. The Janitor knows he is unacceptable as Number One, based on the standards of the group. And, in fact, every time the game is played the Janitor has a preconceived belief that he is automatically Number Eight.

Before the eight volunteers return to the group, I demonstrate what we had really asked them to do. "I wanted you to position yourselves in the order of your importance. And instead of all that dog-eat-dog, King-of-the-Mountain routine, all that was required was for you to all join hands and stand in front of the group in a circle of mutual respect. *For there will never be a person who is more important than any other person, no matter how they look and no matter what kind of work they do. Each of you is as valuable and worthwhile as any other person.*"

That was a new kind of music to their ears, a new and foreign "sit-com" for their eyes. Most kids tell me they've never heard anything like that before, except in church.

Most adults haven't heard it either. Or if they have, it was long ago.

We live today in a narcissistic society. We are struggling to move from the Me generation to a We generation and the going is tough.

The elusive preoccupation we have in self-gratification and self-indulgence has been termed narcissism. The word comes to us from ancient Greek mythology and the story of Narcissus, who fell in love with his own image, reflected in a pool of water. He was the original "If it feels good, do it" guru. Today, narcissism is manifested in redwood hot-tub groupies, designer jeans for tots, too many presents around the Christmas tree, an overt emphasis on youth, sexuality, and physical beauty; and things and places—things to own, things to adorn and places to own and visit; not to share with others, just to show to others.

Don't confuse narcissism with healthy self-esteem.

They are night and day. The word *esteem* means to appreciate the value of. In the human being, I believe it is the beginning and the first seed to all success. It is the basis for our ability to love others and to try to accomplish a worthy goal, without fear. Narcissistic self-gratification is a materialistic, hedonistic type of self-worship. Self-esteem is based on the internalization of spiritual love. Why do we stand in awe of the power and immensity of the sea, the vast unknown reaches of the universe, the beauty of a flower, the splendor of a sunset . . . and at the same time downgrade ourselves? Did not the same Creator make us? Are we not the most marvelous creation of all, with power to think, experience, change our environment and love?

Self-acceptance, as we are right now, is the key to healthy self-esteem—seeing ourselves as worthwhile, changing, imperfect, growing individuals, and knowing that although we are not born with equal mental and physical uniforms—we are born with the equal right to feel deserving of excellence according to our own spiritual standards.

You are a masterpiece of creation. Always carry with you the secret: "Love must be within us before it can be given."

Ten Action Steps to Build Self-Esteem

1. Always greet the people you meet with a smile. When introducing yourself in any new association take the initiative to volunteer your own name first, clearly; and always extend your hand first, looking the person in the eyes when you speak.

2. In your telephone communications at work or at home, answer the telephone pleasantly, immediately giving your own name to the caller, before you ask who's calling. (If no one you don't already know ever calls, forget this part.)

Whenever you initiate a call to any residence or place of business where someone new may answer, always give your own name up front, before you ask for the party you want and before you state your business. The leading with your own name underscores that a person of value is making the call.

3. When driving in your automobile, listen to inspirational radio or cassette tape programs. Automobiles are the best rolling universities in the world. Listen to self-development programs of an educational nature.

4. Invest in your own knowledge. Enroll in an extension or seminar class in some aspect of personal or professional development. Make the bookstores and fitness centers your new haunts for "happy hour."

5. Always say "Thank you," when you are paid any compliment, by any one, for any reason. Neither play down, nor try to play up value that is bestowed. The ability to accept is the universal mark of an individual with solid self-esteem.

6. Don't brag! People who trumpet their exploits and shout for service are actually calling for help. The showboats, braggarts, and blowhards are desperate for attention.

7. Don't tell your problems to people, unless they're directly involved with the solutions. And don't make excuses. Successful people seek those who look and sound like success. Always talk affirmatively about the progress you are trying to make.

8. Find successful "role models" that you can pattern yourself after. When you meet a "mastermind," become a "master mime" and learn all you can about how he or she succeeded. This is especially

true with things you fear. Find someone who has conquered what you fear, and get educated.

9. When you make a mistake or get ridiculed or rejected, look at mistakes as learning experiences, and ridicule as ignorance. After a rejection, take a look at your BAG—Blessings, Accomplishments, and Goals. Look at rejection as part of one performance, not as a turndown of the performer.

10. Spend this Saturday doing something you really want to do. I don't mean next month. *This* Saturday. Enjoy being alive and being able to do it. You deserve it. There will never be another you. This Saturday *will be spent*. Why not spend at least one day a week on You!

Questions about Your Self-Esteem

1. Do you accept yourself just as you are? Would you say that you love yourself?

2. Would you rather be somebody else? If so, why?

3. How do you handle criticism? Do you take it personally or do you seek to learn from criticism?

4. Do you feel guilty when you indulge in some selfish activity? Think of some recent examples.

5. How comfortable are you when others praise or compliment you?

6. Do you talk to yourself with all due respect or with ridicule?

2 | The Seed of Creativity

RELEASING YOUR CREATIVE ENERGY

- You Are What You Watch
- The Second Best-Kept Secret of Total Success
- Your "Robot" Self-Image
- The "Instant Replay" Factor
- How the Viet Nam POWs Survived
- "Doing Within" While You're Doing Without
- Do It Right in Drill!
- How to Master Your Own Creativity
- The Power of Self-Talk
- How to Script Your Own Success
- Ten Action Steps to Creativity

Napoleon once said, "Imagination rules the world." Einstein believed, "Imagination is more important than knowledge, for knowledge is limited to all we now know and understand, while imagination embraces the entire world, and all there ever will be to know and understand."

Among all living organisms on the earth, only the

human being was created without a built-in "software" program for successful living. Insects, animals, and birds know instinctively how they must behave and what they must do in order to survive. Humans also have survival instincts, but we also possess abilities much more marvelous and complex than any animal. Because animals have instincts for daily living that are limited to finding food and shelter, avoiding or overcoming enemies, and procreation, they have no goals beyond survival and security.

The human being, with no prerecorded computer program as a lifeguide, is blessed with a creative imagination. This is why healthy role models and positive family support, superimposed upon a strong spiritual value system, are so important. Since we are not predestined as members of a wandering herd, victimized and imprisoned within a fixed environment, we need maps and charts to guide us. In successful individuals these maps and charts are called role models and values. In unsuccessful individuals they are more like walls and reefs.

All individuals are born without a sense of "self." We are like tape recorders without the key message—with some prerecorded facts and background music, but no central theme. We are like mirrors with no reflections. First through our senses, during infancy—then through language and observation—we tape record, build, and photograph our video, audio, and sensory cassettes of ourselves. This recorded self-concept or self-image—this mental picture of self—when nourished and cultivated, is a primary field in which happiness and success grow and flourish. But this same mental self-concept, when undernourished or neglected, becomes a spawning pond for low achievement, deviant behavior, and unhappiness.

Recently, I heard of a psychologist who gave an intelligence test to a 12-year-old boy. Part of the test consisted of putting pieces of a jigsaw puzzle together.

He tried it, but quickly gave up in frustration, saying: "I can't do it, it's too hard!" His self-image told him that if something looks like a test and you have difficulty with it, then you give up.

Many people see themselves as inadequate. The early messages recorded on their "inner video cassettes" say: "I can't do things very well, especially new things. I don't think people like the way I look. There's no sense really trying, because I'll probably get it wrong and won't succeed anyway." These are the surprisingly large numbers of individuals in this abundant country who have the most difficulty learning and advancing and who are problems to themselves and others.

I have found that the successful people, on the other hand, are those whose "inner video" carries a message something like this: "I can do things pretty well—a variety of things. I can try new challenges and be successful. When things don't go smoothly at first, I keep trying or get more information to do it in a different way until it works out right." These are the individuals who present the fewest problems to anyone, in society, professional life, or in their schools and homes. These are the few who can, and usually do, learn the most and who can share and give the most to others from what they have learned. They have discovered that their imaginations serve as a life-governing device—that if your self-image can't possibly see yourself doing something or achieving something, you literally cannot do it! *"It's not what you are* that holds you back, *it's what you think you are not."*

You Are What You Watch

You have heard the old cliché, "You are what you eat." I would like to offer you a new one to share with colleagues and family members: "You are what you watch and think." A biblical expression in the Book of Proverbs advised us long ago, "As he thinketh in his heart, so is he." Unfortunately, too many people exist on a mental diet of television, motion pictures created to shock us, and slick publications designed to stimulate us. I consider most of what we have available as "junk food" that leads to mental malnutrition and poor emotional and spiritual health.

Television is an extraordinary invention which should greatly improve our lives. Our world has been changed by television. You can turn off the TV set, but you can't turn off television's influence. We have been exposed to a wide variety of cultures and been given insights into life around the globe and in outer space. Television programs bring us athletics, encourage physical fitness, and provide many opportunities for learning about medicine, the arts, economics, local and world news, and religious events. The potential learning opportunities afforded by television programming are unparalleled in the experience of any pre-television generations.

The sad truth, however, is that because of the type of sponsorship necessary to support television in a free market system, very little broadcast time is devoted to stretching our minds, expanding our spirits, and enriching our understanding of ourselves and others. Much of the influence of television is negative. Many programs are dominated by crime, violence, and stereotyped or deviant portrayals of people's lives. A recent study by Harvard University revealed that many adults, as well as children, cannot distinguish between reality and fantasy on television. Children who were interviewed said the things they saw on TV were true because "you can see them actually happening."

Many hospitals have reported patients who requested a doctor whom they had watched on television because that doctor was more familiar with cases like theirs. Every year, TV doctors get thousands of letters from viewers asking for medical advice. When one actor gave a splendid performance as an alcoholic, his wife received dozens of letters of advice and sympathy from women who said they also were married to alcoholics.

If adults have this much difficulty distinguishing fantasy from reality, the effect television has on children is cause for real concern. We all learn by observation and imitation. This is especially true with children. They have a tendency to mimic the individuals they use as role models in their lives, and many of their role models are characters from their favorite television programs. Values are also beamed into children via TV, and many are negative or at the very least, out of touch with reality.

Television constantly exposes children and adults to antisocial behavior performed by the incompetent, the uncouth, and the insane. At the other extreme are the superheroes with unnatural strength and superhuman abilities, who are beautiful and handsome. When average individuals compare themselves to their TV heroes, they usually see themselves as inadequate.

According to the A. C. Nielsen Company, the major broadcast ratings firm in the United States, the average amount of time each individual watches television is over twenty-four hours per week. Children average over thirty hours per week in front of what we commonly refer to as "The One-Eyed Baby-sitter," and they spend more time watching adult programs than children's programs. Preschool children average over four hours per day in front of the TV set and 41 percent are watching between 8:00 and 9:00 P.M. By the time children reach school age they have watched over 20,000 commercials, most of which teach them to consume more and that life's problems can be solved by a certain product in thirty seconds, or less.

We are growing up with television as our "window to the world" and the TV world has become the basis for many of our beliefs and values. By the time we graduate from high school, most of us will have spent

50 percent more time in front of the television set than in the classroom or having quality experiences with our parents and families. We can't really blame the television industry for the situation, because the quality of programming is only a reflection of the character of our families in the American social scene. But let's remember, if a sixty-second commercial, *by repeated viewing,* can sell us a product, then isn't it possible for a sixty-minute soap opera or "smut-com," by *repeated viewing,* to sell us a life-style?

The Second Best-Kept Secret of Total Success

Recent studies conducted by a Stanford University research team have revealed that "what we watch" does have an effect on our imaginations, our learning patterns, and our behaviors. First, we are exposed to new behaviors and characters. Next, we learn or acquire these new behaviors. The last and most crucial step is that we adopt these behaviors as our own. One of the most critical aspects of human development that we need to understand is the influence of "repeated viewing" and "repeated verbalizing" in shaping our future. The information goes in, "harmlessly, almost unnoticed," on a daily basis, but we don't react to it until later, when we aren't able to realize the basis for our reactions. In other words, our value system is being formed without any conscious awareness on our part of what is happening!

What if you and I could switch TV channels to one inside of our own head, in which our minds were cameras instead of receivers? What if we scripted, produced, casted, rehearsed, and broadcast our own programs, and, at the same time, videotaped them for our own enjoyment and for future broadcasts?

Well, we can and we do, every day and night of our lives! And herein lies the second secret:

> **The Second Best-Kept Secret of Total Success is that our minds can't tell the difference between real experience and one that is vividly and repeatedly imagined.**

Understanding this secret of the power of the imagined experience is the fundamental key to understanding human behavior. What you "see" is what you'll get. We perform and behave in life, not in accordance with reality, but in accordance with our perception of reality. Many of our everyday decisions are based upon information about ourselves which has been stored as "truth"—but which is really a combination of hearsay from family, friends, and peers, actual past experiences, and information we read, listen to, and view on television.

Your "Robot" Self-Image

I love the challenge of explaining complex scientific theory and evidence in easy-to-understand ways. Sometimes when I am relaxing at home, sharing mutual experiences with my wife and six children—sometimes one-on-one and sometimes as a group—I make the analogy between the "self-image" and R2D2, the loveable little robot of *Star Wars* fame.

In the first *Star Wars* movie, R2D2 had as his primary goal the hologram (3D) projection of a video cassette, prerecorded inside of him. No matter what happened out in the galaxy, he was driven by his internal guidance system or video cassette. I tell my kids that each of us has his own "self-image robot" in his mind named RUMe2 (Are You Me Too). When we ask ourselves, "Who are you? RUMe2?" the answer comes back, immediately, "Yes I am you, too! I'm the voice inside of you who tells you whether or not you really can do something."

A little poem from my audio album, "The Psychology of Winning," illustrates the point:

My Robot (Self-Image)

I have a little Robot
That goes around with me;
I tell him what I'm thinking,
I tell him what I see.
I tell my little Robot
All my hopes and fears;
He listens and remembers
All my joys and tears.
At first my little Robot
Followed my command;
But after years of training
He's gotten out of hand.
He doesn't care what's right or wrong
Or what is false or true;
No matter what I try—now;
He tells me what to do![1]

During every moment of our lives we program (or we allow others to program) our "self-image robot" to work for us, or against us. Since it is only a process, having no judging function, it strives to meet the attitudes and beliefs we set for it, regardless of whether they are positive or negative, true or false, right or wrong, safe or dangerous. Its only function is to follow our *previous* instructions, implicitly, like a personal computer playing back what is stored—responding automatically.

Much of the video, audio, and sensory information fed into your "self-image robot's" memory stays there. Billions of integrated and separate items of input over a lifetime are all there awaiting retrieval. They can

---

1. Waitley, Denis, *The Psychology of Winning* (Chicago: Nightingale-Conant Corporation, 1979), p. 137.

never be willfully erased by you. You can override them with stronger messages or modify their effects over a period of time, but you own them for life. What has always amazed me is the research reported during brain surgery, in which patients whose brain cells were stimulated with a thin electrode described the sensation of reliving scenes from the past. Their recall was so strong and vivid that all details were there again—sounds, colors, playmates, shapes, places, odors. They were not just remembering, but reliving the experiences!

The "Instant Replay" Factor

When I watch pro football, or any major sporting event, I enjoy seeing it on TV almost as much as I do the excitement and involvement of being there with the crowd. The reason I like sports on TV is because of the fantastic feature of "instant replay" which lets us "relive" the electrifying victory, the incredible come-from-behind upset, and the "big play." The more Howard Cosell, Dandy Don and "The Giffer" replay the "big play," the more I like it. Did you know that college and professional athletic teams that are consistently on top every season, replay the highlights of their best games during the weeks following those games, and during the following season to reinforce their success?

In 1980, I spoke at the awards banquet the night Herschel Walker & Company from the University of Georgia celebrated their winningest football season ever. The following year, when I visited the football players' dorm, it was no surprise to see the returning veterans from the previous year and the new crop of rookies lounging in the TV room, "reliving" an edited collection of the greatest moments in their best season, with their eyes glued to the big TV screen. As I walked toward my Hertz car in the university parking lot for the drive back to the Atlanta airport, I thought of the Second Best-Kept Secret of Success: The mind can't tell the difference between an actual experience and an imaginary experience that is repeated vividly.

As I drove through downtown Athens, I placed a mental bet with myself that "them Dawgs" from Georgia would be on top again. And sure enough, they went undefeated during the following regular season and won the Southeastern Conference. There is a great deal to be said for replaying our past successes, mentally, to make winning more a reflex that comes naturally. There's also a great deal to be said for replaying Herschel Walker in each of those successes—all six-foot-two, 220 pounds of him, with ability to dash 100 yards in 9.1 seconds!

How the Viet Nam POWs Survived

I had the opportunity to interview and study a number of POWs when they returned from Viet Nam, many of whom were Navy pilots who had been shot down by Soviet-made SAM missiles. I also interviewed several of the former hostages after their release from the U.S. Embassy in Iran. Although the POWs endured much more in the way of deprivation and torture, over a considerably longer time period, there is a common seed to their experiences that can bear fruit for each of us. The POWs and hostages who seemed to be in the best physical and emotional condition after their ordeal were the ones who had used the seven years, in some cases, or the 444 days, in others, as a "university without walls."

There was one big drawback to going to class in their "university without walls." All their "university" had was four walls, a cot, and a pot. There were no books—nothing to read, nothing to write with, or paint with, or look at, just the walls. The only light was artificial and that always seemed to be on, deliberately, when it was time to sleep, and off during normal daytime hours. The glaring bulb caused disorientation, fatigue, and distress, precisely the responses desired by prison guards, terrorists, and cult leaders to make their captives more susceptible to their wills.

It didn't take our prisoners of war long to figure out the second best-kept secret of total success. In the absence of any materials, tools, or comforts, they simply created them in their imaginations. They recalled most of the inspirational events and significant learning stored in their memories, which I refer to as "instant replay." And they previewed coming attractions of Emmy Award-winning TV series in their imaginations—every color, every smile, every touch, every word, every picture, every detail. This is the creative ability to concentrate on reinforcing positive, healthy experiences from the past, and to project simulations of a successful project or life-style, as if it were actually happening in the present. This is the gift of creativity.

"Doing Within" While You're Doing Without

Some of our POWs reconstructed well-known passages from the Bible, which became their source of inner strength. Some played golf, by replaying games from memory at their favorite golf courses in previous years. When they tired of replaying old games, they started *preplaying* future tournaments with their favorite PGA pros. They walked the course at Augusta National, with the lush, narrow fairways surrounded by azaleas, trees, and spectators. They felt the excitement of playing in the pro-am with Watson. They studied the break of the putt on the manicured greens. They heard the crowd's approval of their 22-foot birdie on the final hole. And when they were released, back home again in "real life," many were stronger. Amazingly, they returned as better golfers and mentally stronger human beings.

What has impressed me the most about our U.S. POWs in Viet Nam is the ingenious system they had for communicating, even though they were not allowed to communicate. As you may recall, they developed a special type of Morse code, with the alphabet in rows and columns of letters. They tapped on cell walls, pipes, floors, ceilings, sounding at times like a muted clatter of speed typists with a deadline for an important manuscript. The first tap or taps represented the row in which the letter was placed, followed by a short pause, and then a second series of taps to identify the letter by column. For example, the letter A was communicated by Tap (pause) Tap, being in the first row, first column. The letter B became Tap (pause) Tap, Tap. First row, second column. As they mastered this impossible, clumsy way of talking, the speed at which they conversed would rival even the most gifted court reporters.

By pooling their memory banks and imaginations through communication, they remembered hundreds of the most significant passages from the Scriptures to use in their solitary, Sunday worship services. They got to know more about the childhood joys and dreams of the man in the next cell than they will ever know about anyone in their own families; some of these buddies never met each other in person. One pilot, who had particularly excellent recall of his college days, taught a class in aeronautical engineering and thermodynamics, which he had stored in his memory (much to his surprise). They invented hundreds of money-making ideas, built new homes, remodeled their parents' houses, and, alone, whispered "Good night, I love you" to their wives, their children, and their country. But what struck me most is the way they said good night or good-bye to each other. The unmistakable, most familiar tapping cadence of all: "Tap, Tap (pause) Tap, Tap—Tap (pause) Tap, Tap"—GB. "God Bless!"

One of the Iranian hostages took a 444-day train trip in his imagination from London to Bombay. (I'm still trying to figure out how he did it!) He had his own private sleeping compartment with a pull-down bed. He strolled down six car-lengths to the dining car for his meals, and enjoyed the passing scenery as he sipped a glass of port before sunset. He was "doing within," while he was doing without.

In my studies of hostages, POWs, Super Bowl and Olympic athletes, sales and business executives, mothers, fathers, and children, the bottom line is always the same: the replay of success or failure and the preplay of future success or failure. It's interesting to observe that children don't learn how to preplay failure until their parents, peers, and other role models repeatedly show them how. And, also, it's sad to see children and adults who have been taught to dwell on past mistakes instead of using them as learning experiences to reinforce their blessings and accomplishments.

Do It Right in Drill!

When I went through naval flight training, after graduating from Annapolis, I never studied mid air collisions, crashes or perishing in the rugged mountains. We learned precision formation flying, how to recover from a hammerhead stall and inverted spin, and how to survive in subzero weather conditions, with a diet of roots and leaves. I even enjoyed "Dilbert's Dunker," which was a 40-foot slide in an aircraft cockpit into a swimming pool, trapping the pilot. I enjoyed it, until I was told that I was to be the first "trapped pilot" who would try to escape! My first feeble question to the instructor, a Marine major with a scar on his cheek, was, "Has anyone flunked this test before and failed to escape?" He scowled and pointed to the frogmen in scuba gear circling like barracuda in the pool, waiting to move in for the kill. "If you can't pull yourself out, in full flight gear, boots, helmet, and parachute, by releasing the seat belts and shoulder harness, while upside down with your head resting on the bottom of the pool, and swimming the length of the pool underwater to get beyond the burning oil slick—within ninety seconds—the frogmen will bail you out! Do it right in drill and you'll do it right in life," he barked.

As we live day by day, selecting our role models, the television shows the family will watch, what books we will read, which groups we'll join, which memories to harbor, and what kinds of predictions to make, it will help if we think of all these as "drills." Most everyone knows and can recite the historic remark Astronaut Neil Armstrong made when he set foot on the moon: "That's one small step for a man, and one giant leap for mankind." But few have even heard the rest of his radio transmission. He added later: "It was beautiful . . . it was just like we planned it, *just like drill!*"

How to Master Your Own Creativity

In order to master anything, you need to understand how it operates. Although we are only just beginning to comprehend how the brain functions to create the thoughts and automatic emotional and physical responses in each of us, some startling revelations have been made in scientific research that support my own findings.

The real breakthroughs concerning the brain began in the 1960s when Dr. Roger Sperry and his students initiated their split-brain experiments. In these studies, they were able to test separately the mental abilities of the two surgically separated hemispheres of the human brain.[2] They discovered that each half of the brain has its own separate train of conscious thought and its own memories. More importantly, they found that each side thinks in fundamentally different ways, the "left-

---

2. Blakeslee, Thomas R., *The Right Brain* (New York: Doubleday. 1980), p. 6.

RIGHT HEMISPHERE	**LEFT HEMISPHERE**
CONTROLS THE LEFT SIDE OF THE BODY	CONTROLS THE RIGHT SIDE OF THE BODY
NONVERBAL	VERBAL
GESTALT	LOGICAL
INTUITIVE	ANALYTIC
SPONTANEOUS	SEQUENTIAL
FEELINGS	FACTS
ART, MUSIC	LANGUAGE, MATH
SPATIAL	LINEAR
THINKS IN VISUALS	THINKS IN WORDS
HOLISTIC	TEMPORAL

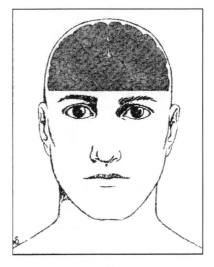

Scientists today agree that the functions of the brain cannot be simply compartmentalized as right- or left-brain. Functions frequently appear in both hemispheres at the same time. This diagram is for general illustration purposes only brain" thinking in words and the "right-brain" thinking directly in pictures and feelings.

Most researchers now concur that the left hemisphere, which controls the right side of the body, contains much of the verbal, logical, and what we generally call conscious functions. The right hemisphere, which controls the left side of the body, functions as the visual, intuitive and subconscious partner. The left-brain handles language and logical thinking, while the right does things that are difficult to put into words. By using images instead of words, the right-brain can recognize a face in the crowd, score high on a video game or put together pieces in a jigsaw puzzle, which would totally frustrate the left-brain.

Let's take, for example, a conversation you're having with another person. Generally, your left-brain responds to the literal meaning of the words it hears and won't even notice the "feeling" or inflection in the voice. The right-brain focuses on tone of voice, facial expression, and body language, while the words are less important. An example of the separate responses in each hemisphere to the same person might be— Right hemisphere: "There's something about him that I don't trust!" Left hemisphere: "Nonsense, the fortune he says we'll make is right here in black and white!"

Most of our "awake" lives are under the conscious control of our left-brain. When we are blessed with a "great idea" or "flash of insight" it seems to arrive suddenly and in a surprisingly complete form. Apparently, it was incubating unconsciously in our right-brain. Mozart and Beethoven said they heard symphonies in their heads, and had only to write them down.

Igor Sikorsky built the first four-engined airplane in 1913 in his native country, Russia. The outsiders said it was preposterous and that it would never fly. When it flew successfully, the left-brain critics said it would never fly high enough and far enough to be of real economic value. He proved them wrong again. When the Communists took over, he had to flee, as did so many creative thinkers, and he arrived in the United States broke but eager to create. He went on to pioneer transoceanic commercial air travel with his Flying Clippers and in his middle fifties developed the helicopter, an invention his American critics said could never fly.

As an eleven-year-old boy, Sikorsky is reported to have had a dream in which he was walking along a paneled passageway, lit by soft blue lights. He dreamed he was inside a big flying ship—one that he had built himself. About thirty years later, he was copilot on one of his big flying boats. His friend Charles Lindbergh was at the controls and Sikorsky decided to take a stretch, walking back into the passenger cabin. In a "flash of insight," he found himself walking along that paneled passageway, inside a big flying ship, lit by soft blue lights!

All you and I need to unleash our creativity is to be "whole brain" thinkers. Thousands of years ago we were more emotional and intuitive. As we learned how to use tools and communicate, we developed into a left-brain society utilizing verbalization, logic, and practical, step-by-step solutions to our problems. The technological progress has been staggering and we seem to have accomplished more during the past fifty years, in terms of scientific breakthroughs, than in all the previous years in our history combined. And this is just the beginning. The computer already is, today, what the electric typewriter was in the early 1960s.

We have a tremendous opportunity for a new Age of Creativity. As the professional and personal computer take over many of our purely routine and mechanical left-brain functions, our time and our minds will be more available. We should be able to experience interpersonal relationships based more on feelings, emotions, and spiritual love than we have in the past. Instead of passively watching television, we can actively visualize and create our own futures, in advance. First, we have to believe we deserve success. Then, we need to visualize and verbalize that success, as if we are script writers for a TV documentary on our own lives. How we write and talk about ourselves today will determine how our plot unfolds tomorrow and the day after tomorrow.

The Power of Self-Talk

You are your most important critic. There is no opinion so vitally important to your well-being as the opinion you have of yourself. And the most important meetings, briefings, and conversations you'll ever have are the conversations you will have with yourself.

As you read, you're talking to yourself right now. "Let's see if I understand what he means by that . . . how does that compare with my experiences . . . I'll make a note of that . . . try that tomorrow . . . I already knew that . . . I already do that . . . pretty good example . . . when are we getting into the 'how to' part?"

I believe this self-talk, this psycholinguistics or language of the mind, can be controlled to work for us, especially in the building of self-esteem and creativity.

Each of us houses two persons: the me I am today and the me I'm going to be, based upon what I hear and see. As we have discovered, we also think in two distinctly separate ways, in two compartments, the left and right hemispheres of our brains.

We're all talking to ourselves every moment of our lives, except during certain portions of our sleeping cycle. It comes automatically. We're seldom even aware that we're doing it. We all have a running commentary going on in our heads on events and our reactions to them. Many of our decisions are subconscious responses in our brain's right hemisphere and since they aren't expressed in words we get a gut-level feeling or some kind of visual or emotional response to what we see, hear, and touch. The left hemisphere verbally criticizes and approves what we consciously say and do. The left hemisphere also verbally abuses the subconscious reflexes caused by the right hemisphere. We see it on the tennis court and fairways every day. "Come on, you klutz, keep the ball in the court," "Keep your head down, you jerk." But it's not your partner across the net or in the foursome who's doing the criticizing. It's one of two partners in your own head! And the right hemisphere knows how to get even with the left. It puts the next drive in the lake, trips you on the tennis court, and gives you a headache and upset stomach just for openers!

You and I are familiar with the *Inner Game of Golf*, the *Inner Game of Tennis*, etc. We know, for instance, how important it is to visualize skiing freely down the fall line, feeling the exhilaration of the crisp air, taking the moguls in stride, skis together, weight downhill. . . . This visualization takes place at home or in the cabin before we ever put the skis on. It is looking at ourselves, in a relaxed mood, through our mind's eye in preparation for the real thing.

Visualization and affirmation of success is sometimes called "scripting." My own theories concerning scripting coincide closely with those held by two of my colleagues, Dr. Thomas Budzynski in the United States and Dr. Georgi Lozanov of Sofia, Bulgaria. Dr. Lozanov's technique, popularly known in this country as "Super-learning," involves deep relaxation, "suggestopedic" music, and spoken words. Dr. Budzynski, a leader in biofeedback research and brain lateralization studies, has developed a learning system called "Twilight Learning."[3] He has discovered that if the left-brain is quieted, the right-brain will hear messages that can transform the body. Both Lozanov and Bud-

---

3. Budzynski, T. H., "Tuning In On the Twilight Zone," *Psychology Today*, No. 11, 1977, pp. 38–44.

zynski believe that when the dominance of the left-brain is suppressed, through relaxation and other techniques of arousal control, the right-brain is also receptive to verbal inputs as well as visual images.

Since most of the negative kinds of feelings, beliefs, and attitudes we have about ourselves are stored, through habitual repetition, in our right-brains we need to start relaxing and using self-talk that is constructive and complimentary, instead of destructive and derogatory.

How to Script Your Own Success

My own approach to positive self-talk is similar to the Lozanov method, although I am using biofeedback techniques with many high-performance athletes. The following is a simplified method that you may find helpful in rescripting your own self-talk for more control over certain aspects of your life:

Choose a time and space in which you won't be interrupted and you can let yourself relax. Physical and mental relaxation are mandatory. The best position is either lying down or seated, with feet uncrossed, back straight and hands loosely at your sides or in your lap.

Turn soft music on the radio, or record player, preferably classical music from the baroque artists (Bach, Handel, Vivaldi, etc.). Select music (if you have a record player or cassette deck) from these baroque artists that is slow in tempo. That will be about 4/4 time, equal to about one beat per second, or sixty beats to the minute. (You'll find your heart rate also may slow down to sixty beats per minute or even slower if you are in good cardiovascular shape.)

Relaxation is the key, but it's helpful to have a cassette tape, which you record in your own voice. This tape consists of self-statements about you, in the first person, present tense, as if you already enjoyed and possessed the qualities which these self-statements describe. You don't have to go to a recording studio. Simply take a blank tape, your portable cassette recorder and go to that quiet place and record your initial tape.

Here are some self-talk statements that I have recorded, in my own voice, for my own health, self-esteem, and creative growth:

My breathing is relaxed and effortless
My heartbeat is slow and regular
My muscles are relaxed and warm
I'm relaxing now. I am at peace
I'm in control of my body, now
I believe I am unique and special
I'd rather be me than anyone else in the
    world
I can feel my body more healthy now
Now is the best time to be alive
I'm proud of my accomplishments and goals
I give the best of me in everything
I keep the commitments I make
I earn the respect of others
All is well with me now
I am reaching my financial goals
I am happy being me right now
My world is opening and expanding
I am at peace. I am at peace
I relish each golden day
I take time for sunsets and flowers
I take time for older people too
I am gentle and giving to my loved ones
I take time to play like a child
I am strong and vital
I'm a winner. I'm a winner
I build other winners too
I respect and appreciate myself
Today is my best day ever
I thank God for the gift of life

When you record your own self-talk (some of which

may be very different from my own examples) speak in a normal voice level. You'll find that the statements will be about four seconds long. Repeat them three times, and alternate speaking in an affirmative voice, a commanding voice, and a softer voice.

After you are relaxed and enjoying the soft music in your own privacy, turn on the cassette of your own self-talk on a portable player. The music should be louder than your recorded voice. Make the self-talk replay just recognizable, but so that it doesn't interfere with your concentration on relaxing to the music. Don't consciously listen to what you are saying on the tape. Let your left-brain take a rest and let your right-brain enjoy the musical interlude. Your right-brain will also record your positive self-talk from the tape, as images and feelings about yourself to support the words.

Your mental picture of yourself is the key to your healthy development. You are the writer, director, and star of either an Oscar-winning epic or a Grade B movie. *Who you see in your imagination will always rule your world*.

You also are your greatest critic. You can devastate your self-esteem and creativity with sarcastic and negative reviews of your daily performance. Or you can elevate your self-image with encouraging and positive feedback and previews of coming attractions. Your self-talk is being monitored and recorded, minute to minute, by your self-image. When you're talking to yourself, watch your language!

Ten Action Steps to Creativity

1. Here are a few characteristics of creative individuals. How many of them fit your personality?
   - Optimistic about the future
   - Constructive discontent with status quo
   - Highly curious and observant
   - Open to alternatives

- Daydreamer, projecting into future
- Adventurous, with multiple interests
- Ability to recognize and break bad habits
- Independent thinker
- Whole-brain thinker (innovative ideas into practical solutions)

2. Are you right- or left-brain dominant?
   a. Is your work space neat and orderly? Your car? Your garage?
   b. Do you prefer to complete one task before starting another?
   c. Do you like to talk things out at the time they occur?
   d. Do you like many varieties of foods, desserts, restaurants and do you eat at a variety of times?
   e. Do you usually watch TV at certain times and prefer a routine of certain programs?
   f. Are your weekends full of new activities and rarely the same?
   g. Do you like art, soft music and jigsaw puzzles? (two of three)

   (If you answered yes to a, b, c, and e; and no to d, f, and g—you may have left-brain dominance. If you answered yes to d, f, and g and no to a, b, c, and e—you may have more right-brain activity.) Any conclusions? No, just more awareness!

3. Don't fall in love with an invention or an idea. Ideas are expendable and there's always a new and better one. Challenge yourself to make them work and get them into practical use.

4. Learn a relaxation technique that works for you. Your creative imagination can be "preplayed" and "replayed" best when you are relaxed, because the left-brain dominance is less intense and the right-brain is receptive to your visual and certain audio suggestions. There are cassette tapes that describe passive relaxation, progressive muscle

relaxation, deep breathing, and biofeedback techniques. Try a few different methods until you find the one you like.

5. When you visualize yourself "in the present" as if you were already accomplishing one of your goals, make certain your visual image is as you would see it out of your own eyes, not "watching you do it" through the eyes of a spectator.

6. Don't scold or berate yourself with left-brain criticism when you make a mistake. Develop an affirmative statement, about five words in length, describing your correct performance, in the present tense. Relax, listen to yourself state the affirmation and visualize the accompanying action and feeling.

7. To recognize and approach problems creatively, it is best to view all problems as "situations needing improvement," "temporary inconveniences" and "opportunities to grow." Change your view or attitude toward problems.

8. Talking about ideas and plans needs to be balanced by trying them out. Theory and practice converge into wholeness. Field-test your ideas.

9. When approaching any decision, consider using the technique which Benjamin Franklin said was his standard method for decision making. Put two column headings on a piece of paper, marked Advantages and Disadvantages. In the Advantages column, list all benefits and positive results you would receive if you go forward with your decision. List all the disadvantages and potential consequences of your decision in the second column. Study the possible impact of the advantages and disadvantages. If the advantages, in your opinion, outweigh the disadvantages, and if you can live with the consequences as well as the positive benefits, then go forward with your decision.

10. Take time out to ride your bike, build sand castles, fly a kite, smell a rose, walk in the woods or

barefoot in the sand. We adults need to explore the wonderful, right-brain world of the creative child within! (Do it this weekend.)

Questions about Your Creativity

1. Do you fantasize and imagine your own success? How recently have you done this?

2. Do you encourage or criticize yourself in your self-talk? Have you made up a brief statement of affirmation to use when your self-talk becomes negative?

3. Do you replay or rehash past failures? Are they more vivid in your "replay" than your successes?

4. Do you replay or reinforce past successes? Do you visualize these successes through your own eyes?

5. Do you see yourself as a real winner in life? How can this attitude help you achieve your goals?

6. How often do you relax and let your thoughts soar? Will you make a date with yourself to do it soon?

3 | The Seed of Responsibility

WE BECOME WHAT WE DO

- **Why the Japanese Succeed**
- **The Third Best-Kept Secret of Total Success**
- **The Disease of Immediate Gratification**
- **Bradford the Barbarian**
- **How to Build Self-Reliance**
- **The Seven C's of Self-Control**
- **Ten Action Steps to Teaching Responsibility**

There's a verse in the New Testament that talks about sowing and reaping. "Whatever we sow, we reap," it says in Galatians 6:7. My grandma taught me a lot about sowing and reaping; but it wasn't only in her garden that she taught me about Seeds of Greatness.

Sometimes we would ride the ferryboat from the Harbor Drive Pier in San Diego to Coronado Island, back and forth all day, for one Indian head nickel each. We'd pack a lunch, take the streetcar downtown, walk aboard and I'd hold my ears until the blast of the horn signaled our departure. When we stood at the bow of the ferry, it was fun to watch the porpoises play tag and hide-and-seek, crossing back and forth like water skiers, just beneath the surface.

The tallest landmark on our trip over was the Hotel del Coronado, with its reddish circular roofs jutting out of the contrasting white wood. My grandma told me about "tent city" which stretched for more than a mile on the Silver Strand beach near the hotel, where hundreds of tourists would arrive in their old Hudsons, Oldses, and Willyses to camp out near the ocean for summer vacation. The polished Cadillacs, Packards, and Nashes were parked at the del Coronado.

She told me that common folk who rode the ferry and camped out in tents knew how to enjoy life more than the people with all the money. I said I supposed so, but later I asked her if someday we could take the streetcar to the del Coronado and maybe look inside the lobby or watch the cars pull in with the guests. She smiled and said, "Perhaps, after the war is over."

On the ferry ride back to San Diego, it would just be getting dark. I would love to look across at San Diego and see the tallest building in the city flash its neon sign on—"El Cortez Hotel." On that particular night, in 1943, there was an air raid drill just as we were returning.

When the air raid sirens would blare, and the lights would go out in San Diego, it was an eerie sight to see the sky suddenly fill with "barrage balloons," which looked like little grey clouds suspended on cables. Actually, they were cranked up from antiaircraft gun emplacements (as our 1943 version of the MX missile), designed to shear the wings off Japanese Zeroes and Mitsubushi bombers and deter a possible invasion of California by sea.

"Will the Japanese beat us in the war and take us over?" I asked my grey-haired grandma, who seemed to have tobacco compresses for every bee sting and wisdom for every question a nine-year-old could pose. "Of course they won't," she reassured, opening the door as we returned to the security of her little frame house. "But they sank our whole Navy and I saw on the March of Times at the Fox Theatre that they are captur. . . ."

"Shhhhhsh, now," she gently interrupted, "they will bring upon themselves what they have put in. They have, by their own actions, sown the seeds of their own destruction." (That might sound like heavy inputs for a nine-year-old to try to fathom, but in my own defense, and hers, you need to remember that in 1943 we were forced to survive without the blessing of television. Our major sources of diversion were discussions, books, radio, and a movie once every couple of months. It was normal for my grandmother to talk with me about life in more adult terms.)

My grandmother went to her room and came back with a handwritten copy of a speech she said she'd seen in a newspaper at her office. The speech had been broadcast on the radio by Madame Chiang Kai-shek. Madame Chiang was the First Lady and the inspirational bulwark of the Chinese people in their struggle against the Japanese armies during World War II.

Grandma sat down and adjusted her glasses. "I didn't copy it all, word for word," she said; then she began reading:

> If the past has taught us anything it is that every cause brings its effect, every action has a consequence. We Chinese have a saying: "If a man plants melons he will reap melons; if he sows beans, he will reap beans." And this is true of everyone's life; good begets good, and evil leads to evil.
>
> True enough, the sun shines on the saint and the sinner alike, and too often it seems that the wicked prosper. But we can say with certainty that, with the individual as with the nation, the flourishing of the wicked is an illu-

sion, for, unceasingly, life keeps books on us all.

In the end, we are all the sum total of our actions. Character cannot be counterfeited, nor can it be put on and cast off as if it were a garment to meet the whim of the moment. Like the markings on wood which are ingrained in the very heart of the tree, character requires time and nurturing for growth and development.

Thus also, day by day, we write our own destiny; for inexorably . . . we become what we do.[1]

Grandma put her glasses down and went into the kitchen to warm the rhubarb pie.

I'll admit I didn't understand too much, forty years ago. But I'm a seasoned gardener now. The truth of those words—the bitter and the sweet—is everywhere.

Why the Japanese Succeed

Through the years and two more wars, I've long since buried any boyhood grudge against Japan, for taking my father from us for those three years and for taking other men, women, and children away from life itself. I have grown to admire and respect the Japanese people, having many Japanese-Americans as close friends and enjoying trips to Japan to learn more of their culture. I ache as much inside for the way that war ended at Hiroshima, as I do for the way it began at Pearl Harbor. It always seems that the innocent bear the effects of leaders' causes.

Not too long ago I was on an airliner going from San Francisco to New York and one section was filled with Japanese visitors, in a tour group, on their way to

---

1. Nichols, William, *A New Treasury of Words to Live By* (New York: Simon & Schuster, 1947), p. 14.

experience "The Big Apple" for the first time. I was impressed with their ability to break out of their own language into English, without much difficulty. Of course, English is a required subject in Japan; whereas foreign languages are becoming more and more optional, and less and less mandatory in our own school systems.

I overheard two smartly dressed ladies in the group talking to each other in understandable English. They had decided to try to communicate as we do for the duration of the trip. I wasn't purposely eavesdropping as I heard them chatting and quipping across the aisle in front of me. "What do you want to do, first, after we arrive at Kennedy?" one of them inquired. "Get off the plane and get our baggage," teased the other.

"No," the other laughed, "I mean after we check into the hotel." "I don't really care," came the reply. "I'd like to look in all the stores and shops for gifts to take back home. I have heard that prices are much more reasonable here in America." "But we must be a little careful," her friend cautioned. "The prices are lower, but the quality is not what it should be."

I stuck my nose back in my *Wall Street Journal* and swallowed hard, feeling just a little tug inside my stomach walls. These young Japanese women were not being sarcastic or flippant. They were simply expressing honest opinions, based upon their own perceptions. I thought back to my exposure to Japanese products as I was growing up. In those days, "Made in Japan" meant the items were mainly wood and paper kites, parasols, fans, matches, boxes, and other curiosities. Almost all Japanese imports were relegated to five-and-dime stores because of the questionable quality of workmanship.

Today, when I look for the Hudsons, Studebakers, Nashes, Willyses, Kaisers, and Packards that I used to see parked at "tent city" when I was a boy, I keep counting more Datsuns, Toyotas, Hondas, and Izusus. I have been giving motivational seminars recently to

American car salesmen throughout the country. One particular morning I was really pouring on the productivity message. As I stomped across the meeting room platform, I told the three hundred salesmen that I was "bullish" on the rekindling of the great American tradition of excellence and dedication.

"Gentlemen," I boomed authoritatively, "we have gone full circle. We are now on track again and are gaining momentum toward a full economic recovery."

And I concluded with even more rich resonance in my voice, "Gentlemen, we can see the light at the end of the tunnel!" A voice in the crowd shot back, "Yeah, and it's a Japanese freight train coming the other way!"

It seems incredible, doesn't it, that a country small enough to fit easily into California in terms of size, could crawl out of the rubble of World War II and become one of the top two economic powers in the world in less than forty years. Of course, we helped Japan rebuild its factories and economy. But there's much more to this story than a beneficent uncle. Among nations, Japan has the lowest infant mortality rate, the highest percentage of literacy, the longest average life span, the highest education level among youth, and it is among the lowest in violent crimes of any nation. Overpopulated and underresourced, Japan still comes on like an undaunted David taking on Goliath.

In fairness to the rest of us in the Western world, we must point out that centuries of inbred culture have had a significant influence on Japan's industriousness and resilience. Their standard decision-making process is referred to as *nemawashi* (wrapping roots of a tree or bush together, before moving it); a free translation might be "circular agreement." Agreement is necessary *throughout* each organization, at every level, before action is undertaken in Japan. This is cumbersome and can be frustratingly time consuming, but it certainly reduces the likelihood of disgruntled employees and strikes. A successful tool the Japanese employ in their *nemawashi* style of management is the "quality circle" designed to involve small, diverse groups of staff and line employees who meet regularly to discuss work-related problems. Ironically, the "quality circle" concept was developed by an American, W. Edward Deming, in 1948. Since its successful implementation by the Japanese, American companies have begun to rediscover this group communication device in an effort to counter lagging productivity.

Perhaps the major factor responsible for the success of the Japanese in "building greatness out of ashes" is their willingness to look ahead to the future, while putting in a maximum effort of work and sacrifice in the present. Japanese workers save an estimated 20 percent of their spendable incomes, more than triple that of Americans. In Japan, it is called "discretionary" income, which means there is a choice to spend it or save it. In America, we call it "disposable" income, and when we get it, we hasten to dispose of it!

The Third Best-Kept Secret of Total Success

It seems obvious to everyone but us, as individuals, that we Americans are disposing of our past rewards at a greater pace than we are replenishing our investment today for future harvesting. Instead of simply resting on our laurels, we may actually be engaged in pawning them.

As a society, we protest for individual liberty and social order in the same breath. We strive for material wealth and would like spiritual wealth as a by-product. We plead for more protection from crime, but demand less interference in our social habits. We want to cut taxes, take the great risk, and build our own destinies and at the same time we want more financial security and safety provided by our government. But we can't have it both ways. If we want results we must pay the price.

> **The Third Best-Kept Secret of Total Success is that our rewards in life will depend on the quality and amount of the contribution we make.**

We want freedom, but are we willing to pay that price any more? I believe you and I are. That's why I wrote this book. It is my way of looking in the mirror, at my life, and my family's life, and saying to myself, "Come on, wake up America! Let's hitch up the wagon and move out again. If God gave us the Law of Cause and Effect so that we could take stock of how we are faring, we can take advantage of it by studying the "Effect" of the way we live. The secret is in changing the "Cause."

The Cause of most of our social problems consists of many separate smaller causes. I have traveled nearly every day for the past four years, interviewing students at every grade level, parents, politicians, astronauts, former hostages and POWs, Olympic athletes, business executives, and factory workers. The same message comes through loud and clear. "Responsibility needs to be redefined and retaught to this and all upcoming generations." Nothing shouts louder of a nation's condition than the habits of its youth. And the habits of the youth of America are nothing more than a direct reflection of how adults handle responsibility.

The record needs no embellishing. As you read this book, *every fifteen seconds* a traffic accident involving an intoxicated teenage driver will take place, bringing injuries to others. Every twenty-three minutes one of our children dies in an automobile crash and in most cases, drugs or alcohol is involved. This year, of the several hundred thousand American young people who try to commit suicide, over five thousand will carry out the act. Over 80 percent of these suicide victims will have made open threats before they followed through. Suicide is now the second leading cause of death among teenagers, with traffic accidents ranking first. What is causing this onslaught of violence and tragedy?

The Disease of Immediate Gratification

The culprit is disguised in a six-word slogan: "Relief is just a swallow away." The greatest single cause of what's ailing America, in my opinion, is the "irresponsible obsession with immediate sensual gratification." We want love without commitment. We want benefit packages without production requirements. Pain, sacrifice, and effort are unacceptable. If it feels good right away, I'll try it. If I can't be certain to win, then I won't enter. I want the American dream I saw on TV, in the movies, and the one my parents said I'd get because I'm so special. And I want it now. Tomorrow is too late!

In his compelling book, *Me: The Narcissistic American*,[2] which I highly recommend to all parents and leaders, psychoanalyst Aaron Stern brilliantly pierces to the heart of the problem:

> To attain emotional maturity, each of us must learn to develop two critical capacities: the ability to live with uncertainty and the ability to delay immediate gratification in favor of long-range goals.
>
> Adolescence is a time of maximum resistance to further growth. It is a time characterized by the teenager's ingenious efforts to maintain the privileges of childhood, while at the same time demanding the rights of adulthood. It is a point beyond which most human

---

2. Stern, Aaron, M.D., *Me: The Narcissistic American* (New York: Ballantine, 1979), pp. 28, 55.

beings do not pass emotionally. The more we do for our children the less they can do for themselves. The dependent child of today is destined to become the dependent parent of tomorrow.

As the father of six children, I know from experience that the greatest gifts that parents can give their children (and that managers can give their employees) are roots and wings. Roots of responsibility and wings of independence. When those roots and wings are missing, the results are very disturbing—even tragic.

Bradford the Barbarian

In my parenting and leadership seminars, I tell a true story about a young couple who invited me to their home for dinner some time ago after an all-day program at a university. This man and woman, both highly intelligent, with advanced degrees, had opted for a "child-centered" home so their five-year-old son Bradford would have everything at his disposal to become a winner out there in the competitive world. When I arrived at their driveway in front of a fashionable two-story Tudor home at the end of a cul-de-sac, I should have known what was in store for me. I stepped on his E.T. doll getting out of the car and was greeted by, "Watch where you're walking or you'll have to buy me a new one!"

Entering the front door, I instantly discovered that this was Bradford's place, not his parents'. The furnishings, it appeared, were originally of fine quality. I thought I recognized an Ethan Allen piece that had suffered "the wrath of Kahn." We attempted to have a cup of hot cider in the family room, but Bradford was busy ruining his new Intellivision controls. Trying to find a place to sit down was like hopping on one foot through a mine field, blindfolded.

Bradford got to eat first, in the living room, so he wouldn't be lonely. I nearly dropped my hot cup in my lap in surprise when they brought out a high chair that was designed like an aircraft ejection seat with four legs and straps. (I secretly visualized a 20-millimeter cannon shell, strapped to a skyrocket under the seat, with a two-second fuse.) He was five years old, and had to be strapped in a high chair to get through one meal!

As we started our salads in the dining room, which was an open alcove adjoining the living room, young Bradford dumped his dinner on the carpet and proceeded to pour his milk on top of it to ensure that the peas and carrots would go deep into the shag fibers. His mother entreated, "Brad, honey, don't do that. Mommy wants you to grow up strong and healthy like Daddy. I'll get you some more dinner while Daddy cleans it up."

While they were occupied with their chores, Bradford had unfastened his seat belts, scrambled down from his perch, and joined me in the dining room, helping himself to my olives. "I think you should wait for your own dinner," I said politely, removing his hand from my salad bowl. He swung his leg up to kick me in the knee, but my old ex-pilot reflexes didn't fail me and I crossed my legs so quickly that he missed, came off his feet, and came down hard on the floor on the seat of his pants. You'd have thought he was at the dentist's office! He screamed and ran to his mother, sobbing, "He hit me!" When his parents asked what happened, I calmly informed them that he had fallen accidentally and that, besides, "I'd never hit the head of a household!"

I knew it was time to be on my way when they put Prince Valiant to bed, by placing granola cookies on the stairs as enticers. And he ate his way up to bed! "How are you ever going to motivate him to go to school?" I asked quietly. "Oh, I'm sure we'll come up with something," they laughed. "Yes, but what if the neighborhood dogs eat what you put out? He'll lose his way just like Hansel and Gretel!" (I asked the Lord for forgiveness for not remaining silent, as I drove back to the airport.)

As a traveling lecturer, I see many children who are in charge of their parents in America today. I also observe many teenagers and adults who, as a result of low self-esteem and poor leadership, are out of control. If you are interested in the best documentation of irresponsibility in our society today, I urge you to preview the film *Epidemic*, produced by MTI Teleprograms, Inc., in Northbrook, Illinois.

One-third of our children start smoking marijuana in grade school and one in ten high school seniors smoke it every day. And this is nationally, not just in certain regions of the country. There are three million teenage alcoholics in America, and the number is growing. Now I'm not a right-wing or radical, and I don't cry "Wolf!" easily. But we've got to speak up on these issues! Pot is the number one agricultural business in California, Florida, Georgia, and I don't know how many other states. And it is not harmless! On the contrary, THC, the psychoactive ingredient in marijuana, can cause permanent memory loss and many serious problems in our reproductive systems. Based on recent government research, pot smokers are starting to show up with lung cancer in a pattern similar to smokers of regular cigarettes. It all adds up to self-destructive behavior based upon parent, peer and media pressures for immediate sensual gratification.

How to Build Self-Reliance

Our true rewards in life will depend on the quality and amount of contribution we make. From the Scriptures, to science, to psychology, to business, the documentation is the same. "As we sow, we reap." "You shall know them by their works." "You get out what you put in." "For every action, there is an equal and opposite reaction." "There's no such thing as a free lunch."

The way we can build self-reliance is to recognize the number of alternative choices we have in a free society. When I interviewed our returning POWs and the former hostages from Iran, the thing they said they missed most of all was their "freedom of choice." There are two primary choices in our lives: to accept conditions as they exist or to accept the responsibility for changing them.

A recent University of California at Berkeley study indicates that the happiest, best-adjusted individuals in their present and older lives are those who believe they have a strong measure of control over their lives. They seem to choose more appropriate responses to what occurs and to stand up to inevitable changes with less apprehension. They learn from their past mistakes, rather than replay them. They spend time "doing" in the present, rather than fearing what may happen.

The opposite type of individuals believe in luck, fate, jinx, wrong time and the wrong place, astrological and biorhythm accuracy, and "you can't fight city hall." They are prone to give in to doubt and fear and suffer greater emotional and physical problems as a result. They see themselves as victims of the system. And they believe you either have it or you don't and that most success is a lottery or a roll of the dice. When we analyze what the Japanese have accomplished since World War II; when we read of the thousands of achievements by individuals who have walked out of the "ghetto" into greatness, we realize the truth. In America, many victims of the system are actually volunteers who are cooperating in their own failure.

In Chapter 1 we talked about the three great fears: fear of rejection, fear of change, and fear of success. One good way to conquer fear and build more self-reliance is to realize that we all are "God-created, but self-molded," and that we are given love, spiritual leadership, divine rules, and laws to help us understand how we cause our own effects by our decisions.

I've learned to look for constructive feedback even in the harshest ridicule of my beliefs. I've learned that failures should be looked at as "stepping-stones to success." From the hostages and POWs, I've come to cherish my freedom and the responsibility it carries. I enjoy exercising the many choices I have to respond to the many challenges I face.

To build our own self-reliance we need to replace fear with knowledge and action. I recently read a University of Michigan study that has helped me reduce the part that fear plays in my life. The study determined that 60 percent of our fears are totally unwarranted; 20 percent have already become past activities and are completely out of our control; and another 10 percent are so petty that they don't make any difference at all. Of the remaining 10 percent of our fears, only 4 to 5 percent are real and justifiable fears. And even of those, we couldn't do anything about half of them! The final half, or 2 percent of our fears which are real, we can solve easily if we stop stewing and start doing . . . knowledge and action.

Here is a formula. It seems simplistic on the surface, but has some real merit when you try it. There are 365 days in a year. Of all of the fears that you now feel, or ever will feel, only 2 percent of them are a legitimate cause for concern and attention. Why not nip them in the bud early? Since 2 percent of your days in a year are "fear" days, you will be legitimately worrying about seven days per year. Since most of us take about three weeks' vacation every year from our daily routine (and our fear), this gives us forty-nine weeks to absorb seven days of fear!

Here's the recommendation: Pick one day, every seven weeks, and mark it with a big red F in advance on your calendar (after you read this chapter). Although, initially, it will be your "fear in disguise" day, it will really progress to mean "follow-through" day.

Concentrate that one day, in seven weeks, on identifying all the sources of current and potential worry and anxiety in your world. Write down those current and future concerns, and list some alternative choices you have in dealing with them. Next, either telephone, arrange a personal interview with, or write someone you respect or someone you have been referred to as "one who may shed light on your problem." Start getting feedback. If you'll take one specific action on each fear listed, you'll discover that your "F" day, even if it's an hour or two out of that day, will sharpen your advance and contingency planning. And when fear comes begging for attention, you will have already taken positive steps to minimize its impact, forty-nine days ago!

We are not only self-incarcerated victims of our own fears; we are victims of habit and group conformity. In a very real sense, each of us becomes a hostage of hundreds of restrictions of our own making. As children, we either accepted or rejected the environmental "uniforms" handed us by our parents. As teenagers and young adults, some of us had a strong need to conform to the standards of our peers. While we fooled ourselves into thinking we were being "different," we actually were as regimented as any army calling cadence and marching in full dress uniform.

To be self-reliant adults, we need to set some guidelines.

Be different, if it means higher personal and professional standards of behavior.

Be different, if it means being cleaner, neater, and better groomed than the group. It is always better to arrive for any function looking slightly better, than slightly worse than the others.

Be different, if it means to put more time and effort into all you do.

Be different, if it means to take the calculated risk. The greatest risk in life is to wait for and depend upon others for your security. The greatest security is to plan and act and take the risk that will make you independent.

The Seven C's of Self-Control

Are there some specific steps toward being different? Indeed there are. I call them "the Seven C's of Self-Control":

1. **We Control the Clock.** Yes we do. Although it always runs, we can use it as we choose. We can choose how long we work, how long we play, how long we rest, how long we worry, and how long we procrastinate. We can't always set our work schedule, but we can in the long run. We can change. To control the clock better—get up a half hour earlier and decide what you are going to do with the day that is profitable to you and those close to you. Make phone calls at certain times, allow incoming calls at certain times, be available for meetings at certain times, handle each piece of correspondence just once and delegate all work that can't stand up to the test of "is this the best use of my time right now?"

2. **We Control our Concepts.** We control our thoughts and creative imaginations. We need to remember that imagination, with simulation, leads to realization. Ask the POWs if anyone could control their previews of coming attractions.

3. **We Control our Contacts.** We can't select all the people we'd like to work with and be with; but we control whom we spend most of our time with and we can meet new people. We can change our environments and seek out successful role models to learn from and share with.

4. **We Control our Communication.** We are in charge of what we say and how we say it. Realizing that nothing is learned while we talk, much of our com-

munication is listening, observing, and qualifying. When we communicate (you and I) we are prepared to deliver a message that will offer value and mutual understanding on the part of the receiver.

5. **We Control our Commitments.** We choose which Concepts, Contacts, and Communications warrant the most attention and effort. We are responsible for which of them become contractual, with priorities and deadlines. We create our own track to run on—slow, medium, or fast—in our commitments.

6. **We Control our Causes.** With our Concepts, Contacts, and Commitments, we set our long-range goals in life, which become our causes, the things we are most identified with by others. You and I have worthy causes and a game plan for life, which gives us confidence and courage.

7. **We Control our Concerns.** Most people react emotionally to everything they interpret as a threat to their self-worth.

   Because you and I have a creative self-image and a deep-down inside feeling of self-worth, regardless of what's going on around us—we respond, rather than react—using left-brain logic combined with right-brain intuition. And our responses usually are constructive. What concerns us most is the joy of living.

We realize that we are responsible for causing our own effects in life. We tackle the toughest, most challenging assignments in our lives first, understanding that our gratification will come after we have made the effort to do the job. We tell our employers what we are going to offer them in the way of service, before we ask about the pay scale and benefit package. We are well aware that our true rewards in life will depend on the quality and amount of contribution we make. In the long or short run, we reap what we sow.

Ten Action Steps to Teaching Responsibility

It begins early. . . .

1. When children are old enough to understand, they should put away their own toys, play materials, eating materials, and bathing materials. They should be responsible for making their beds, and keeping their personal belongings in order as a regular routine. Never pay children for doing something for themselves; in so doing, it actually robs them of self-esteem and is a form of bribery.

2. Responsibilities should be set for each family member; for operating the home (which later becomes the business) there should be regular chores, at certain times on certain days. Payment may be in the form of strokes, allowances, or special privileges. Whatever is done should be checked, approved, and paid for on a relative scale, similar to that which will be encountered away from home. Preteens and teens should have savings accounts and/or checking accounts, and should go in person to open them and make withdrawals. Dream lists should be encouraged and posted in a prominent place. Children should be encouraged to save their money for very special dreams they have had for three to six months minimum, and even longer if possible.

   It continues. . . .

3. Television should be off unless eyes are on it. Programs should be selected from the TV schedule as to their value, interest, and plot. Alternate forms of diversion should be planned: plays, books, concerts, recitals, museums, seminars, educational video cassettes, walks, talks, ghost stories, games—anything to stimulate the creative imagination and get control. When controversial shows are watched on TV they should be discussed, dur-

ing commercials and afterward, with all views listened to, rather than challenged. Television should not go into the right-brain, subconscious of a child, teen or adult, without at least a logical review.

4. Until your teens fly the nest, it is your responsibility to know where they are, who they are with, pretty much of what's going on and when they'll be home. Any friend should be welcomed to your home. The best way to know what kind of environment your kids are into is to invite the peers over and observe, firsthand. The second way is to meet the parents of your children's friends. Set rules that both parents will enforce. Set them in advance with your kids, and ask the kids what penalty would be fair for breaking the rules. The penalties kids assign themselves, if they're involved in the process of rule-setting, are usually a lot tougher than the parents assign. Be consistent in your demands and in your discipline.

5. Do not buy your children an automobile. If you must, after they have saved for the down payment, cosign a note at the bank to guarantee that they will pay it back. Kids should make their own car and insurance payments. Cars that are given by parents get condemned at least three years earlier to the junk pile than cars purchased by the kids; a kid who buys his own car polishes it twice as often. If there is any evidence of any use of alcohol or drugs connected with your teens' or young adults' use of an automobile, automatically take action for a three- to six-month period. *A teenager dies every twenty-three minutes in a car crash!*

And it continues, all throughout life. . . .

6. Carry the motto with you in all your teachings: "Life is a do-it-yourself project." When your sub-

ordinates bring you a problem, you should ask them first, "What do you think we should do about it?" When you give suggestions, be certain to give the responsibility for the solution and follow-through back to the subordinate. Resist the temptation to take the easy way out and do it for them.

7. Don't talk about drug abuse and irresponsibility, and come back late from a three-margarita lunch. Never preach what you don't practice.

8. Become a role model for your peers and those you want to lead. And always model yourself after people you respect. Don't model yourself after the group in which you run. I saw an entire sales staff who smoked the same brand of cigarettes as the marketing manager (and it was a health care insurance firm!).

9. Let your children, employees, and subordinates make mistakes without the fear of punishment or rejection. Show them that mistakes are learning devices that become stepping-stones to success.

10. Never make excuses for anything. If a commitment can't be met, always call immediately with the reason. Never make excuses after the fact. Procrastination of any decision leads to the rationalization of failure. Never make excuses to the people you are leading.

Questions about Your Responsibility

1. What is holding you back most in achieving more success? What can you do about it?

2. Do you live with a lot of "have to's" in your world?

3. Do you feel in control of your destiny? In what areas of your life are you postponing gratification to reach long-range goals?

4. Do you give more than you are expected to give? Think of a couple of specific instances where you did so recently.

5. Are you a victim of many external circumstances? How could you use those circumstances to help teach responsibility to someone else?

6. How can you better control what happens to you? To help you answer, do a quick review of the "Seven C's."

4 | The Seed of Wisdom

WHAT IT MEANS TO LIVE "WITHOUT WAX"

- The Integrity Triangle
- Knowledge Makes the Difference
- To Thine Own Self Be True
- If I Could Live My Life Again
- The Fourth Best-Kept Secret of Total Success
- Ten Action Steps toward Wisdom

In ancient Rome being a sculptor was a popular profession. You were not really considered to be in the mainstream if your home or place of work didn't have several statues of the gods adorning it. As with every industry, there was good and bad quality in the statue business. When, upon occasion, a sculptor would make a mistake in carving a particular statue, the crack or chipped area would be filled with wax. Sculptors became so good at "remodeling" with wax, that most people could not tell the difference in quality with the naked eye.

If anyone wanted an authentic statue of fine quality, carved by someone who took pride in his work, he would go to the artisan marketplace in the Quad in Rome and look for the signs at the booths marked *sine cera*—without wax. In the *sine cera* booths he would find the real thing.

In everything we do in life we are looking for those items and for those individuals who represent the real thing. More than any other virtue we look for in people, we value "sincerity"—without wax.

In the previous chapter, I described responsibility as understanding God's great law of cause and effect. This chapter is devoted to wisdom, which is the combination of honesty and knowledge applied through experience. Wisdom is honest knowledge in action. There is no greater example of the law of cause and effect than that which is demonstrated in the results of a person's honesty or dishonesty, over a period of time. There can be no real success without honesty. Someway, someplace, sometime, somehow, the person or house of wax will melt to reveal the fraud inside.

I have already referred to Earl Nightingale as, in my opinion, one of the greatest philosophers of our time. Earl gave me my start in the personal development field when he took the time to listen to a single audio cassette recording that had been taped from an evening lecture I had done at a church in San Diego. Earl sent the tape to his partner, Lloyd Conant, in Chicago and the result was my "Psychology of Winning" album, which was my first major success as a self-help program.

Even before I met Earl in 1973, I had been a great fan of his via the radio. Since then I have had the opportunity to listen to most of his radio shows, playing the records and tapes for my own education and listening enjoyment. Listening to Earl Nightingale must be, for me, what listening to Bach and Beethoven is for the classical music connoisseur—pure pleasure. In relistening to Earl's insights into human nature, I find one single thread that is woven throughout the fabric of most of his programs. That common thread is personal honesty.

Earl Nightingale calls our personal honesty "The Unfailing Boomerang." I have always said that "who you are goes full circle" and that is exactly what a boomerang is designed to do. Every time individuals engage in dishonest activities of any kind the results come back to haunt them. When a politician runs for a major office, his or her backers try to anticipate "skeletons in the closet" of the past that can come full circle during a campaign or during a term of office.

It is a sad commentary that many of our retail businesses must resort to lie-detector tests, in advance, to help select honest clerks and employees. In the United States today, expediency has replaced honesty and integrity as the major consideration. If you have the money and the source, you can buy term papers on any high school or university subject; you can hire a "surrogate" to take a final for you; and you can buy a bachelor's, master's or doctor's degree. You cannot, however, buy respect and a reputation. They are not for sale. They are forged with honesty. They do not melt under the heat of inquiry, or the test of time. They are without wax.

More than any other quality, honesty is what I most want in my six children. If taught early, we never seem to lose it. It becomes part of our being, part of our way of doing things; and, more than anything else, it virtually guarantees our success in life as human beings.

If you found a wallet full of money on the sidewalk, what would you do? You would be surprised at the variety of answers I get from the audience during my seminars.

"It depends on how much money is in it."

"I'd keep it and run an ad in the paper for a week, and if it wasn't claimed, I would spend it."

"I would keep the money and send the wallet back to the owner."

If you or I found a wallet of money on the sidewalk, we would contact the owner based upon identification in the wallet and return the wallet and money intact. We would expect no reward other than a thank you. Isn't that what we would hope for if we had lost our wallet? Of course. We seek honesty in our relationships by volunteering it in all of our own actions. Even if we don't receive honesty in return in most of our daily transactions, as long as we never waver from our own deeply rooted values, the score will add up in our favor in the long run. This is one of the most basic, most obvious and, unfortunately, least understood principles of life. Good actions get good results in time.

The Integrity Triangle

My children range from preteens up to mid-twenties and are all trying to grow personally according to their own internal standards of excellence. None of the six is experiencing problems with alcohol, drugs, low self-esteem, hostility, depression or lack of motivation. All of them are asking questions about real integrity, standards of conduct, career direction, financial posturing, and realistic expectations.

In my professional seminars and in our home discussions, I try to simplify the process of personal honesty because it is so fundamental in its nature. As a model for testing ourselves on a daily basis, we can use what I call "The Integrity Triangle." It consists of three basic questions that we can ask of any decision:

1. Is this true?
2. Is this what I believe I should do?
3. Is what I say consistent with what I do?

These three questions make up the points of the triangle because they involve consistently thinking, doing, and saying what you believe to be true. The base of the triangle has one additional question, which you consider after you are satisfied that you can be consistent on the three points. The base question, which keeps the triangle standing, is: "What is the effect of this decision going to be on the others involved?" This base question involves knowledge and understanding as well as integrity.

It is not enough to think the truth, act the truth, and speak the truth, although to be able to do these in concert is to succeed in life. To be effective human beings, we also must consider the impact of our decisions on other people in our lives. The ability to anticipate the probable effects of our decisions on other people's lives, as well as on our own life, is what I consider to be wisdom. When we honestly consider the well-being of others, before we decide to profit ourselves, we become truly rich in the deepest sense.

Knowledge Makes the Difference

According to the UCLA Brain Research Institute, the potential of the human brain to create, store, and learn may be virtually unlimited. The prominent Soviet scholar, Ivan Yefremov, has told the Soviet people: "Throughout our lives we use only a fraction of our thinking ability. We could, without any difficulty whatever, learn forty languages, memorize a set of encyclopedias from A to Z, and complete the required courses of dozens of colleges."[1]

If this is true (and it is), why don't most people learn more and accomplish more in their lifetime? One obvious but painful reason is that they don't believe they

---

1. Nightingale, Earl, "Our Changing World" (radio program), Nightingale-Conant, Inc., Chicago. August 1974.

are worth that much time and effort. This is why low self-esteem is such a devastating growth inhibitor. However, I believe the major reason they don't learn and accomplish more is that they are too lazy to make the effort. People have an aversion to doing more than is absolutely necessary to get by.

The only way we can obtain knowledge is through study. Study for most people is like paying taxes or going to the dentist. It is something people do not like to do and something few people will do if it is not absolutely mandatory. Most people believe that graduation day is the end of study. The United States has the most abundant supply of free educational materials in the world. Our libraries and university extensions are bulging with enough data on every subject to make anyone who is willing to spend the equivalent of one-half hour per night, both intelligent and successful. This is a primary reason the Japanese are outstripping us as the top economic and scientific country in the world. They place a much higher priority on continuing education. They produce ninety-five percent of the television sets we use to while away our hours of apathy and boredom.

Peter Drucker, the famed management expert, advises us that "Today, knowledge has power. It controls access to opportunity and advancement. Scientists and scholars are no longer merely on tap, they are on top. They largely determine what policies can be considered seriously in such crucial areas as defense or economics. They are largely in charge of the formation of the young. And the learned are no longer poor. On the contrary, they are the true capitalists in the knowledge society."[2]

As the computer replaces the typewriter, calculator, and filing system in the information revolution, more

---

2. Drucker, Peter, *Age of Discontinuity* (New York: Harper and Row, 1968), pp. 372, 373.

and more power will be vested in those individuals possessing knowledge and mental ability. Just as the industrial revolution catered to line managers with manufacturing and materials experience, so is the information revolution calling for "intellectual entrepreneurs" with strong technical and financial educations.

While I was affiliated with the Salk Institute for Biological Studies in La Jolla, I enjoyed attending lectures given by the late Dr. Jacob Bronowski, the brilliant mathematician and philosopher, who wrote *The Ascent of Man*. I still have my notes from one of his lectures in which he pointed out that: "knowledge is not a looseleaf notebook of facts. It is a responsibility for the integrity of what we are. You cannot possibly maintain that informed integrity if you let other people run the world for you, while you yourself continue to live out of a ragbag of worn-out information from old beliefs."[3]

To Thine Own Self Be True

Our lives are made up of many thoughts, actions, and emotions. Our thoughts and our experiences continually form a memory bank which we try to organize and utilize effectively. We differ from one another mainly in the depth and clarity of the organization of our knowledge.

Socrates, one of the wisest individuals who ever lived, believed that "knowledge is the one good; and ignorance is the one evil." He also believed that each of us should cultivate a strong individual character and many personal virtues.

William Shakespeare interpreted our individual differences and our responsibility for recognizing those differences when, in *Hamlet,* he had Polonius say,

---

3. Bronowski, Jacob, *The Ascent of Man* (Boston: Little, Brown and Co.), 1973, p. 436.

"This above all: to thine own self be true, and it must follow, as the night the day, thou canst not then be false to any man." Shakespeare did not mean "if it feels good, do it." He really meant that "when in Rome you don't have to do as the Romans do!" We should live according to our deep spiritual convictions, our integrity, and our social conscience. This is being true to ourselves, while respecting the rights of others.

All of us yearn to seek our destinies and spend our lives in our own ways. However, most of us find ourselves in the same dilemma from the time we reach our teens throughout the major part of our adult lives. How do we really want to spend our lives? What shall we choose to do? What can we do that will fill our lives with meaning and bring us the adventure and rewards we are looking for? How do we know we have selected the right career or the proper goals?

These are heavy questions. They should not be taken lightly. We should not let the first paying job we take out of high school or college determine our profession for the rest of our life. We should not let our parents, our professors or our friends decide which career path we should take. We should not let economics alone make our long-range decisions. Before we can be true to ourselves, there is a first step. Before we can set meaningful goals or develop a purpose in life, there is a starting point. It is like the chicken and the egg. Most people begin with the chicken, which is a job. Success can be better assured if we start with the egg, which is knowledge. Most people are better prepared and motivated in their hobbies than they are in their lifework.

If I Could Live My Life Again

In my goal-setting seminars, I include a dream session called "If I could live my life again." It is designed to allow us to consider why and how we should think about achieving some of our dreams. As people write out their "If I could live my life again" statements, they consider possibilities that they haven't explored as yet. Every time this session is completed, I am amazed at the number of people who, while sincere, have ended up with a job they really didn't want.

When I first read *Your Natural Gifts* by Margaret E. Broadley, I knew I was onto something significant in the personal and professional development field. My only regret is that I did not meet her when I was fifteen. I met Margaret Broadley and her publisher, Evelyn Metzger, in Washington, D.C., in the fall of 1982, following a reception at Vice President Bush's home. As a result of that meeting, I have decided to record an audio cassette album, based upon her book, which I believe should be required listening for all sophomores in high school and their parents. It should be required listening not because I am recording it, but because Mrs. Broadley's research into *Your Natural Gifts* can change people's lives significantly, for the better.

Margaret Broadley's writing concentrates on the marvelous research efforts conducted by the Human Engineering Laboratory of the Johnson O'Connor Research Foundation. For over half a century, the O'Connor Lab has been dedicated to the discovery of natural inborn talents and to learning how these "gifts" usually are expressed or neglected in today's workplace.

When I finished reading *Your Natural Gifts*, I knew I had found a missing link in my own personal and professional development seminars. I had been traveling around the world for ten years telling people that winning is all in the "attitude." I had been playing the game without a full deck of cards. I had placed too little emphasis on the need for self-understanding of natural abilities. Both Jonas Salk and Hans Selye had given me friendly warning that the so-called motivators preached too much about attitude, without properly weighing "aptitudes."

Johnson O'Connor was convinced that much of the frustration, depression, and restlessness in society is related to aptitudes that are not being used or properly expressed. I believe that O'Connor and his human engineers are right on target. My research, my own experience, and my observations of my six children corroborate the need to learn what we are "good at," rather than try to model our lives after individuals who possess completely different talents from our own.

In my own case, I have always felt an affinity for verbal expression, foreign language, poetry, philosophy, and human relations. I have expressed little ability or interest in engineering, structural visualization, mechanics, and the physical sciences. I graduated at the top of my class from La Jolla High School in 1950, with scholarly opportunities to Stanford and other major universities. However, the Korean War had just begun and I and my classmates were interested in serving our country. Rather than enlist in one of the services, I began to consider a military scholarship so that I could continue my education, while committing myself to officer candidate school and a tour of active duty thereafter.

My dad and I used to love to listen to football games on the radio. The year before I graduated from high school we started watching the games on our new "miracle" Grundig television set. Our favorite game was Army versus Navy, with Arnold Tucker handing off to "Mr. Inside" and "Mr. Outside"—Felix "Doc" Blanchard and Glenn Davis. While we were watching one particularly exciting game, my dad told me his dream of all dreams was for me to graduate from West Point or Annapolis. Hearing my dad say that gave me early determination. I became obsessed with making his dream come true.

I graduated from the United States Naval Academy at Annapolis in 1955. Academically, it had been a struggle for me to make it through the four years. Whereas I had been a straight A student in high school, I found myself like a fish out of water at the Academy, which was primarily oriented toward the mechanical and marine engineering studies. I stood at the top of my class in English, foreign language, and after-dinner speaking. I wrote and directed a musical comedy that received enough acclaim to warrant its inclusion on "The Ed Sullivan Show." However, that was an extracurricular hobby activity, with no place in a naval career. What is significant is that I graduated at the bottom of my class in mechanical engineering, electrical engineering, and advanced calculus, the most important subjects in preparation for my new career as a carrier-based Navy attack pilot. To please my father, I had, unwittingly, put myself on a fast track leading away from my "natural" talents.

Reflecting on the past twenty-five years of my life, I am eternally grateful to my parents for their sacrifices and encouragement in my pursuit of education and wisdom. My nine-year career as a naval aviator was stimulating and rewarding. It taught me more about self-discipline, goal-setting and teamwork than I possibly could have learned in any other profession. The real point I am trying to make is that it has taken me a quarter of a century to reshape my life into expressing those talents that I really have in a profession that I truly enjoy. Today, to me, work is play. I can hardly wait to wake up in the morning and learn more about the way we think and behave. My wife Susan and I have made it one of our primary goals in our lives to help our children discover their own natural abilities so they can blend these talents with acquired skills and knowledge to achieve maximum satisfaction in their individual lives.

Susan and I have been introducing our six children to a variety of educational and cultural activities to stimulate their interest in identifying careers and avocations. One by one, we have been encouraging them to explore their natural gifts through tests conducted by the Johnson O'Connor Research Foundation Laboratory, which are available to the general public. I have found the tests so fascinating and revealing, that I decided to take them myself.

The tests measure nineteen separate aptitudes:

1. *Personality*—whether objective and suited best for working with others, or subjective, belonging more in specialized, individual work.

2. *Graphoria*—identifies clerical ability in dealing with figures and symbols.

3. *Ideaphoria*—creative imagination or expression of ideas.

4. *Structural visualization*—the ability to visualize solids and think in three dimensions.

5. *Inductive reasoning*—the ability to form a logical conclusion from fragmented facts.

6. *Analytical reasoning*—the ability to resolve an idea into its component parts.

7. *Finger dexterity*—the ability to manipulate fingers skillfully.

8. *Tweezer dexterity*—the ability to handle small tools with precision.

9. *Observation*—the ability to take careful notice.

10. *Design memory*—the ability to remember designs easily.

11. *Tonal memory*—the ability to remember sounds and express an ear for music.

12. *Pitch discrimination*—the ability to differentiate musical tones.

13. *Rhythmic ability*—the ability to maintain a set rhythmic timing.

14. *Timbre discrimination*—the ability to distin-

guish sounds of the same pitch and volume from each other.

15. *Number memory*—the ability to store many things in your mind at the same time.

16. *Proportional appraisal*—the ability to distinguish relative and harmonious proportions.

17. *Silograms*—a test for the ability to learn unfamiliar words and languages.

18. *Foresight*—the ability to look ahead prudently.

19. *Color perception*—the ability to distinguish colors.[4]

Don't let the terminology turn you off as to the practical value of these tests in your daily life. This kind of self-analysis is not reserved for the intellectually inclined or supereducated people. The tests have been conducted for individuals in all walks of life, from students to fast-food service workers, from entertainers to presidents of large corporations. Even a president of the United States has tested himself for his "natural" gifts.

I discovered that I, indeed, am strongly oriented to a career calling for strong ideaphoria, analytical reasoning, observation, silograms, and verbal abilities. I also discovered that I have unusual natural talents related to music. One of my sons discovered these musical gifts of his too, as did my wife. None of us has ever pursued any form of music as a vocational or hobby pursuit, although each of us admits to a suppressed desire to play an instrument. Writing lyrics and songs comes naturally to me, but, somehow I never took the time or effort to develop my skills in this field.

---

4. Broadley, Margaret E., *Your Natural Gifts* (McLean, Virginia: EPM Publications, Inc., 1972), pp. 3–9.

One reason it is so important to identify natural ability is that the lack of one important talent may frustrate and thwart an entire career. One young man could not follow in his famous surgeon-father's footsteps because he hesitated too much during simple surgical procedures. What his father falsely branded as cowardice actually was the lack of tweezer dexterity! Structural visualization is also a prerequisite for individuals desiring to become surgeons.

Before fathers set their hearts on sons following in their footsteps as surgeons, they would be well advised to check their sons for structural visualization aptitude, while they are still in high school. Structural visualization is not passed on from father to son. It is inherited by sons from their mothers only! Daughters can inherit structural visualization from both mothers and fathers. It may be better for surgeons to look more to their daughters to carry on the great family tradition!

While natural abilities are important, it would be dangerous and irresponsible to suggest that we should base our career orientation on nothing more than a series of aptitude tests. Our careers are a blend of natural abilities, environmental modeling, acquired skills, and experience. Many times our careers hinge heavily on the economic requirements at pivotal age and family considerations. If we are to develop our lives along the path of greatest wisdom, however, we should give serious thought to discovering our inherent abilities as early as possible.

Even if we decide to pursue our natural gifts as hobbies, diversions, and extracurricular activities, we will be more fulfilled and satisfied if we are able to express our talents creatively and regularly. Many of our frustrations lie deep within us. We cannot even explain them to those we love. We can only say with helpless acknowledgement, "I don't know why I feel that I am wasting my life, but I do."

The Fourth Best-Kept Secret of Total Success

A powerful fact in this chapter came to me as the result of my research into aptitude testing and its real value in determining the success people experience in their everyday lives. Human engineering research over fifty years indicates that one of the most important "aptitudes" for success also is a mystery to 95 percent of the world's population.

The Fourth Best-Kept Secret of Total Success is that a large vocabulary—which implies broad, general knowledge—characterizes the more successful persons, regardless of their occupations.

Knowledge is the frontier of tomorrow. Brain is becoming more and more the master of brawn. Our struggle for physical survival may not be as crucial now, and in the future, as our ability to survive and coexist intellectually amid all of the "fallout" of our technological progress. One of the major problems we have in trying to work with each other toward mutually beneficial solutions to our problems lies in our ability, or inability, to express our thoughts in words. Frustration with this inability often results in physical violence. While violence has been increasing each year, the nation's vocabulary level has been decreasing approximately one percentage point each year over the same period.

Regardless of education, most people use only about four hundred words in more than 80 percent of their everyday conversation. Although there are over 450,000 words in an unabridged English language dictionary, we use the same words over and over again. If we were to learn only ten new words each day for one year, we could become among the most learned and well-spoken individuals in the world.

It should please you to know that reading is the best way to gain knowledge and a greater vocabulary. Only 5 percent of the people living in the United States will either buy or read a book this year. As you continue to learn you will gain more knowledge about your natural talents and the skills you can develop to take advantage of them. As you read, you will be able to express your ideas more clearly. You will identify and seek out the best role models to help accelerate your success. The more education you receive, the happier you will become.

As Thomas Wolfe summed it up in *The Web and the Rock*: "If we have a talent and cannot use it, we have failed. If we have a talent and use only half of it, we have partly failed. If we have a talent and learn somehow to use all of it, we have gloriously succeeded, and won a satisfaction and a triumph few individuals ever know."

You and I know that wisdom depends not so much on the number of words we know, but how we use them to express ourselves to others. It also depends on the honest assessment of our talents and the determination to use them to the fullest. We apply this wisdom to our children and our associates. We live this wisdom every day. Never stop reaching!

Ten Action Steps toward Wisdom

1. Continue your education regardless of your age. Studies indicate that older adults do 10 percent better in college classes than their younger student associates.

2. When you read, always keep a dictionary beside you to look up a new word you don't completely understand. By looking up the meaning on the spot, it easily can be part of your vocabulary forever.

3. Get a good vocabulary primer. Only approximately 3,500 words separate the average person from those with the best vocabularies. Read to your children at very early ages (even prior to their first birthday). They will assimilate more than you can ever imagine. Encourage your children to read more than they watch television.

4. Consider taking a reputable aptitude test. Check to see if the Johnson O'Connor Foundation has an office near you, or check with your favorite library or university.

5. Before you make a decision, ask yourself: "Is this the honest thing to do? How will it affect the others involved?" You can't go wrong with this test.

6. Check the aptitudes of your children by their sophomore years in high school. By the eleventh grade, they should be deciding which college or trade school or first job they are going to pursue. By checking and encouraging their natural gifts, you are giving them a "fishing pole" they can use to fish with for the rest of their lives. Don't pass your career goals on to your kids, unless they have determined that they want to enter your chosen field.

7. Think, say, and do what you believe is true, consistently, in all of your transactions.

8. Get a library card for yourself and for every member of your family. Books are the fountain of wisdom. They take us where we can't go in person.

9. Don't overlook correspondence courses, continuing education seminars, and night or weekend classes. There also are audio and video home study courses which are outstanding. I know a man who got a master's degree in his car going to and from work. I know a lady who got a business

degree via television, while she was doing her housework and caring for her small children.

10. Model yourself after people you most admire and respect. And above all, set an example of integrity and sincerity for your children and subordinates. Live your life as one of the *sine cera* artisans— make sure your model is the real thing, sculpted without wax!

Questions about Your Wisdom

1. Are you honest with yourself and others? How would two persons who know you well answer?

2. Do others trust you completely? Recall one recent instance in which you proved yourself trustworthy.

3. Are you going where you want to go, doing what you want to do, and becoming who you want to become?

4. If you could live your life over again, who would you be? Write it out.

5. Are you making the best use of your real talents in your profession? How will you find expression for those talents?

6. What are you doing to expand your vocabulary and your knowledge? Which of these will you do next week:—Obtain a library card?—Buy or borrow a book and begin reading in an area of your interest?—Start a vocabulary-building program?

5 | The Seed of Purpose

THE GOLD MINE IN YOUR GOALS

- **The Fifth Best-Kept Secret of Total Success**
- **Eric Showed Us How**
- **The Power Within**
- **The Guardian of Your Mind**
- **"Hi Ho Kheemo—Away!"**
- **The Wheel of Fortune**
- **How to Mine Your "Goal Mind"**
- **The Awesome Power of Suggestion**
- **Ten Action Steps toward Your Goals**

Remember in *Alice in Wonderland,* when Alice comes to the junction in the road that leads in different directions and she asks the Cheshire Cat for advice?

"Cheshire-Puss . . . would you tell me please, which way I ought to go from here?"

"That depends a good deal on where you want to get to," said the Cat.

"I don't much care where____" said Alice.

"Then it doesn't matter which way you go," said the Cat.

The grinning feline spoke words of truth, didn't he?

If we don't know where we want to go, then any road will take us there—and it doesn't really matter what we do in life.

According to the U.S. Department of Labor, only three out of every one hundred Americans reach age sixty-five with any degree of financial security. Ninety-seven out of one hundred Americans who are sixty-five and over must depend on their monthly Social Security checks to survive. Is this because the American dream is shattered? Is it because of runaway inflation? Is it because the OPEC cartel controls our energy supply and causes business recessions in the West? All of the world economic conditions have an effect on our personal lives. It is more difficult to survive and thrive during harsh recessions and artificially stimulated recovery cycles, in which the value of the dollar is eroded. There are, however, *internal* considerations that I believe are equally as relevant as the environmental circumstances.

Would it surprise you to learn that only five of every one hundred Americans, who are in the higher income professions such as law and medicine, reach age sixty-five without having to depend on Social Security? I was astounded to learn that so few individuals achieve any degree of financial success, regardless of their level of income during their most productive years.

Most people live their lives under the delusion that they are immortal. They squander their money, their time, and their minds with activities that are "tension relieving," instead of "goal achieving." Most people work to get through the week with enough extra money to spend on the weekend.

The Fifth Best-Kept Secret of Total Success

Most people hope that the winds of fate will blow them into some rich and mysterious port of call. They look forward to when they can retire *Someday* in the distant future, and live on a fantasy island *Somewhere*. I ask them how they will accomplish this. They respond *Somehow*.

The Fifth Best-Kept Secret of Total Success is that the reason so many individuals fail to achieve their goals in life is that they never really set them in the first place.

In the goal-setting seminars I have been giving throughout the United States and internationally, it is obvious that the majority of people spend more time planning a Christmas party or a vacation than they do planning their lives. By failing to plan, they actually are planning to fail by default.

In one of my recent seminars, I divided two hundred participants into groups of six attendees each. They sat at circular tables and wrote down and discussed their personal responses to each part in a series of five questions. The questions I asked were these:

1. What are your greatest personal and professional abilities and liabilities?
2. What are your most important personal and professional goals for the balance of the year?
3. What is a major personal and professional goal you have for next year?
4. What will your professional level and annual income be in five years?
5. Twenty years from now:
   Where will you be living?
   What will you be doing?
   What will you have accomplished, that could be written or said about you by family or peers?
   What state of health will you enjoy?
   What will be your assets in dollars?

After the groaning and grumbling had subsided, the mastermind groups went to work discussing the most important topics they could ever share. As difficult and unreasonable as these questions may appear, you must remember that these two hundred people each paid fifty dollars to attend a goal-setting workshop. They seemed dumbfounded that someone actually was challenging them to think about their own lives in specific terms. It was fun to sit and listen to the stories of people crawling out of the ghetto into greatness. But it was no fun to consider doing it yourself. That sounded like being back in school!

Eric Showed Us How

As the groups of six got started, I noticed the boy. Eric had red hair and looked about ten. I thought it was a good move for his father to bring him along for some positive exposure on how the adult world operates. He had listened carefully while I had talked, and now he had come up to ask me what the people were doing at the circular tables. I explained that I had given them a series of five questions about their goals in life to discuss in small groups and then come back later and discuss them with the entire seminar audience.

He mentioned that many of them looked like they were talking about other things and that some of them were just laughing and telling jokes. I told him that we couldn't expect everyone to take this goal-setting exercise seriously, because many people thought that setting goals was like trying to decide whether to watch TV or go to a movie. He asked me why I wasn't working on my goals at one of the tables. I said that mine were pretty well defined and that it might be fun for him to copy the questions off of my notes and try to answer them for his own life. He took one of my yellow-lined pads and a pen and began writing earnestly. When the forty-minute time period was over, I called the small groups back together for the debriefing session.

Question number one had been fairly easy. As I had anticipated, abilities such as "good with people," "sensitive to the needs of others," "dedicated" and "honest" were stated most frequently. Liabilities such as "need to organize time and priorities better" and "want to spend more time on self-improvement projects and more quality time with family" also were brought out. These were standard answers from every group.

However, 90 percent of the whole group seemed to find questions two through five difficult—if not impossible—to relate to. Goals for the balance of the year (question two) were "to do better than last year," "to make more, get more, save more and do more" and "to be a better person." The same kind of general, noncommittal answers were offered to question three concerning goals for the coming year.

The real problems came with questions four and five. When asked what their professional levels and incomes would be in five years they almost all hedged, using the same excuses: "Who can predict in these uncertain times?" "It depends on the inflation rate." "That's up to my boss and the company." Most of them did admit, however, that they expected to be at a higher level of employment and earning more money five years from now.

Question five was the real mindblower. In twenty years—where, what doing, what accomplished, how healthy, and what assets? They agonized, giggled, and hollered. One middle-aged man volunteered that he would probably be dead by then. The audience chuckled. Chuckling relieves tension. Most of the group had never considered the question before and came up with inane, nonsensical answers. They said they would be millionaires with yachts anchored off the Isle of Scorpios, or have written famous novels, or have their own TV series. In almost every group the response was the same. No one wanted to forecast or predict his or her own future. They were like all the other groups I had taught, with one exception—the boy named Eric.

When Eric volunteered to come up to the podium and read his answers to the series of five goal-setting questions, the seminar audience was delighted. They looked forward to more laughs and games. I wasn't certain what to expect, but I figured he couldn't be any more wishy-washy than the adults.

"What are your greatest talents and what would you like to improve most, Eric?" I began.

He didn't hesitate. "Building model airplanes and scoring high in video computer games are my best things and cleaning my bedroom is what I should do better."

I moved on quickly to his personal and professional goals for the rest of the year. He said his personal goal was to complete a model of the Columbia space shuttle craft and that his professional goal was to earn about four hundred and fifty dollars mowing lawns and later shoveling snow. The audience murmured their approval. *Now we are getting someplace,* I thought to myself.

I asked him what his personal and professional goals were for the coming year. He answered that his personal goal was to take a trip to Hawaii and that his professional goal was to earn seven hundred dollars so that he could pay for the trip. I asked him for more details about the trip. He said it would be during summer vacation, to Honolulu and Maui, on Western or United—whoever had the best package. I asked him what the hardest part would be in reaching the goal of that trip and he said it would be getting his mom and dad to save enough for their tickets, so that they could take him.

We moved on to Eric's five-year goals. When I asked him about his professional level and income in five years, he still did not hesitate. "I'll be fifteen, and I'll be in the tenth grade in high school," he stated clearly into the microphone. "I plan to take computer courses, if they have any, and science classes. I should be earning two hundred dollars a month, at least, in a part-time job," he stated confidently. The audience wasn't chuckling any more. Even Eric's dad seemed genuinely interested in what the ten-year-old had in mind for this "Fantasy Island" game.

Eric had to think a moment as he considered my question about twenty years from now. He started, "I'll be thirty years old then, right?" I nodded and he continued. "I'll be living in Houston or Cape Canaveral, Florida. I'll be a space-shuttle astronaut working for NASA or a big company. I will have put new TV satellites into orbit and I'll be delivering parts for a new launching station in space. And I'll be in great physical shape. You have to be in good shape to be an astronaut," he concluded proudly.

It was fantastic to hear Eric talk in specifics, whereas all of the adults talked in circles. The impact of what he had said was slowly sinking into the seminar participants. They had paid fifty dollars each to come and sharpen up their goal-setting skills. A ten-year-old guest had come up and demonstrated how it should be done. The critical difference in Eric was that he hadn't begun to believe that he couldn't achieve his goals. Enough rain had not fallen to ruin his parade. He hadn't watched the evening news enough, or read the paper enough yet. He hadn't taken enough personal defeats. He was unspoiled, uncynical. His "weakness" of inexperience was his greatest strength.

Eric's thoughtful answers supplied me with one of the best conclusions I have ever had to an all-day seminar. This redheaded kid had accomplished more in ten minutes than I had in five hours of talking. He had taught us that we *can* talk about our dreams in much more specific, concrete terms if we won't allow our cynicism to stand in our way. Eric, a ten-year-old boy, had given us all a living example of how goals should be set and pursued.

The Power Within

Eric's perception as a ten-year-old is testimony that the human being is goal-seeking by design. My favorite analogy is one that was taught me by my friend—the late Dr. Maxwell Maltz, plastic surgeon and best-selling author of *Psycho-Cybernetics*. Dr. Maltz compared the mind to the homing system in a torpedo or an automatic pilot. Once you set your target, this self-adjusting system constantly monitors feedback signals from the target area. Using the feedback data to adjust the course setting in its own navigational guidance computer, it makes the corrections necessary to stay on target. Programmed incompletely or nonspecifically—or aimed at a target too far out of range—the homing torpedo will wander erratically around until its propulsion system fails or it self-destructs.

The individual human being behaves in very much the same manner. Once you set your goal, your mind constantly monitors self-talk and environmental feedback about the goal or target. Using this negative and positive feedback to adjust your decisions along the way, your mind subconsciously makes adjustments to reach the goal. Programmed with vague, random thoughts or fixed on an unrealistic goal too far out of sight, the individual will wander aimlessly around until he gives up in frustration, wears out, or self-destructs.

Have you ever known individuals who hadn't adequately prepared themselves for either reaching or managing their goals? Did they blow a great opportunity or relationship? Did they give up and cop out in frustration? Did any of them self-destruct? I see this type of behavior more and more in our society as we search for immediate sensual gratification in a world that still only bestows long-lasting rewards on those who work for them. When people learn that there are few if any shortcuts to success, many of them cannot cope with the disappointment. Their parents did not teach them how to live with this sort of frustration.

What is the power within—the driving mechanism—that moves us toward our dominant thoughts? We have learned that the subconscious self-image probably dwells in the right hemisphere of our brains and that it can't tell the difference between an event that really took place and one that was vividly imagined (Chapter 2). It appears that once the self-image receives a message with enough frequency, that message will become a habit that we accept as part of us.

Have you ever stopped to think about your habits? How many do you have that you really don't want, or that are not good for your mental and physical health? Smoking, drinking, overeating, being late, nail biting, feeling depressed or cynical—these are all subconscious habits that are learned. All of them suggest a self-esteem problem and usually require self-image modification to bring about any permanent change. The only other possibility for immediate change is for someone to tell us: *If you don't stop doing it you are going to die!* Even with this threat, many people can't find the power within to change.

But we can change if we want to. In my work with prisoners of war, astronauts, Super Bowl champions, executives and their families, I have seen an obsession that was a flimsy cobweb of an idea at first—through long hours of practice and effort—solidify into something as tangible and worthwhile as an Olympic gold medal. We all have the power within. There is a potential gold mine inside each of our goals.

The Guardian of Your Mind

You and I are different from most people because we genuinely expect our dreams to come true. We are interested in improving our lives and the lives of those we touch. We are not fanatics. We do not fall for bizarre or fad notions, potions, or lotions. We want to understand how we think and why we do things. We want to learn enough about how our mind functions so we can get it to work for us, rather than against us. One mechanism in your brain you should understand is called "the guardian of your mind."

Radiating from your brain stem is a small network of cells, about four inches in length, called the "reticular activating system." It is just about the size and shape of a quarter of an apple. I like to refer to it as your own built-in "Apple" computer.

The reticular activating system performs the unique function of filtering incoming sensory stimuli (sight, sound, smell, and touch) and determining which ones are going to make an impression in your mind. It decides, from moment to moment, what information is going to become part of your world.

How many people do you know who won't listen to reason? Do you have any friends who say they want your help, but continue on a failure track? Have you seen or heard of individuals who always seem to be looking for trouble? Of course, you see them every day. What they do not realize is that they have tuned their reticular activating systems to guard their minds against success by deliberately seeking the negative inputs and problems they say they are trying to avoid. By considering, so often, the possibilities of failure, their brains have been set up to operate as failure-seeking homing torpedoes!

Stop reading this book for a moment. Sit quietly and listen carefully to all the sounds around you. It's interesting, isn't it, how you are able to concentrate on reading without being aware of all the distractions. The "reticular activating system" filters out the unimportant stimuli and focuses on what is important at the moment. The sound of a crying child, a siren, or the ring of the telephone, would cause you to pay less attention to the book and direct your awareness to the sound you heard. Once you have made a distinction that a certain value, thought, idea, sound, picture, or feeling is significant to you, your reticular activating system is alerted. It immediately transmits any information it receives regarding this significant item to your consciousness.

To illustrate clearly how the "reticular activating system" works for you, let's imagine that you recently purchased a home near a busy commercial airport. Your reasoning behind the purchase was that you work all day during the week and are home only during the evenings, which is when air traffic is significantly reduced. You also have figured that with the extra money you have saved by purchasing a less expensive home in the airport landing pattern, you will buy a small cabin cruiser on which to spend your weekends. You have decided to tolerate some noise and vibration in return for some financial rewards.

Shortly after you move into your new home, you are certain that you were insane at the time you purchased it. Every fifteen minutes the windows shudder, the furniture shakes, and the whine of jet engines gives you an "Excedrin headache." Upon analyzing the situation, however, you conclude that it is important to your financial future that you stick it out for at least two years. Within a few weeks an amazing transition begins to occur. You are able to sleep better at night. The landing noise becomes more like the soft murmur of the ocean. You don't seem to notice the windows rattling and the table shaking. Your "reticular activating system" has gone to work blocking out the unimportant information, helping you concentrate on your priorities.

You decide to invite some friends over to your home for dinner several weeks later. They live up on the hill, out of the traffic pattern, but only a mile or two away. As you sit down at your dining room table, a DC-10 makes its normal approach directly overhead. The dishes vibrate and the hanging light fixture sways. Your guests are completely unnerved. "How can you stand living here?" they moan. "Oh, you mean that airplane noise?" you answer honestly. "Yes," they reply, looking at each other. "How often do you have to go through this?" "We hardly notice it any more," you respond. "We are bothered more by those motorbikes roaring up the dirt trails by your house!" Your friends respond as you knew they would. "Roaring motorbikes? What motorbikes? We don't hear any motorbikes by our house any more. They went somewhere else a long time ago," they conclude, emphatically.

The beautiful feature about the reticular activating system is that you can program it to be on the alert for success-related inputs. It will wake you up in the morning without an alarm clock. If it knows you are looking forward to another eventful day, it will get you right out of bed. If it knows that you are looking for values and qualities in other individuals, it will home in on values and qualities. If you are seeking more financial rewards, it will be extremely sensitive to any financially-oriented data that could help you.

The reticular activating system explains accident-prone people, as it conversely explains success-prone people. It explains why some people see a problem in every solution, and why others see a solution for every problem. Some people are cursed with an "Apple" computer in their brains that they have programmed to find the worst in everything. Because we are programming ourselves to be positive, you and I are blessed with an "Apple" computer that looks for the best in every situation. Be careful what you give importance to in your thinking and in your conversations with others. Your reticular activating system is recording everything and it will turn your desires or fears into your goals. Concentrate your attention on *where you want to go*, not *away* from where you don't want to be. You will always move in the direction of your currently dominant thoughts.

"Hi Ho Kheemo—Away!"

My children are learning early about the power of goal-setting. They don't completely understand the reticular activating system, but they do grasp the idea that you always move toward your dominant thought. I'll never forget what happened after my daughter, Dayna, who was about eleven at the time, attended one of my goal-setting seminars. She was unusually quiet as we drove home. She had something brewing in that pretty little head.

Several days later I noticed strange occurrences around our household. I stubbed my toe on what appeared to be a heavy metal Frisbee lying hollow side up in the kitchen. "Who put this land mine in front of the refrigerator?" I howled at my kids, who were eating Count Chockula cereal with sliced bananas on it. Dayna answered brightly, "I did, Dad. That's my dog's dish."

"How can that be your dog's dish, when we don't have a dog?" I retorted, knowing this was some kind of put-on (we have a history of ingenious practical jokes that we perpetrate on each other to keep the family alert).

"He's my imaginary dog, Dad. But he's becoming so real that I had to buy his dish this week, so we can feed him when he gets here!" she blurted excitedly.

"Let me pour cold water on this dog-goal of yours in a hurry," I scolded, swallowing a spoonful of bananas and cereal. "That dish is big enough for a horse and, besides, we're not getting a dog right now, period."

She came right back at me, "But you said if you really set your mind on something and get all the information on it then. . . ." I interrupted her as parents normally do. "I know what I said," I answered, "but that was at the seminar, and we're home now. Children can't set their own goals without the prior consent of the great goaltender, and that's me!" The children ate their cereal in silence, packed their lunches, kissed their mother good-bye and went to school.

When I came home from a meeting that Saturday afternoon, I saw Dayna walking around the yard talking to a long chain that she was dragging behind her in one hand. I interrogated her as soon as I walked out of the garage. "What are you doing talking to yourself with that piece of chain in your hand?" I inquired. "It's not a piece of chain, Dad," she corrected me. "It's my dog's leash and I'm practicing taking him for a walk." I told her to practice in her room because the neighbors might be watching and they thought we were a bit strange already.

I knew I'd been a little gruff with my kids on the dog issue, so I decided to smooth things over and humor my daughter a little by appearing to be interested in her goal. "If you did get a dog, at some future date when we move, what kind of dog would you get, honey," I inquired softly. "Yorkie or poodle?"

"You know I don't like little lapdogs, Dad," she sighed. "My dog's a malamute."

My recollection of malamutes was that they are large dogs, with huge appetites, and that they are designed to pull sleds in the Arctic. I reminded her that we lived in Southern California where it was balmy all year, and that the poor dog would pant and shed its fur, seeking shelter under a tree all summer long. "And besides," I added, "he probably would smell!"

She had a one-track, monorail mind. "You're right, Dad," she replied, "malamutes have great noses. He'll always find his way back home and he'll be a great watchdog, you'll see."

The situation was getting desperate, but I knew I held the "hole cards" in the form of the checkbook and the absolute veto power when I was outvoted in family council meetings. "If you did get this dog, which you won't for a year or so, do you know approximately what he would look like?" I asked Dayna after dinner. Her answer caught me a little off guard.

"He's got a black fur coat, with brown on his tummy and upper legs," she said admiringly. "He has a white diamond on his forehead and beautiful brown eyes," she beamed. She pulled out a little pocketbook titled *The Care and Feeding of Malamutes* and flipped through the pages. "You'll learn to love Kheemo, Dad," she said confidently, reminding me of myself when I tried to convince the children that squash and cauliflower were delicious.

"What do you mean, Kheemo?" I said, trying to control the irritation I was beginning to feel with this impossible "wishful thinking."

"Kheemo is his name, Dad," she sighed, "it's an abbreviation for the name Kheemosabee (*Kheemo-sah-beh*), which is an Indian expression meaning 'good friend.' " I reminded her that I grew up listening to the Lone Ranger every week on the radio and that I was well aware of the expression that Tonto used to greet his friend, the masked man. Feeling that we had reached an impasse in the discussion, I broke off the dog debate and we went in the living room to join the other members of the family.

The next day was Father's Day. I should have realized it was going to be a special day all right. I had been set up by my own children for the payoff on the very day they were supposed to honor me.

I came down the stairs that Sunday morning determined to spend the kind of Father's Day I had always fantasized. I came to the breakfast table in my pajamas, robe, and slippers, with the *TV Guide* in one hand and the morning paper in the other. "Today, we're going to the second service at church and afterwards, I'm going to concentrate on doing absolutely nothing," I announced to the family. "I'm going to get back in my bathrobe, relax, and watch baseball and old movies all day," I added, with a touch of arrogance. I noticed that the kids were all dressed, with their hair combed and their jackets on, as if they were going on an outing. I opened my Father's Day card and taped at the bottom, after all the endearing poetry, was a classified ad from the morning paper:

> Last of the litter. One adorable AKC male Malamute puppy. Pure-bred, papers, shots.

Only $500. Drive by today. This one won't
last. Ideal children's pet.

"Don't you want to take your children for a drive
after church on Father's Day?" the little darlings
chimed in together.

"As a matter of fact, that's exactly what I don't want
to do," I retorted, sticking my nose in the *TV Guide* to
see what time the game came on. Their response, obviously well rehearsed and probably coached by their
mother, sounded like something out of Harry Chapin's
classic song "The Cat's in the Cradle."

"That's OK, Dad, don't be blue, 'cause we're gonna
grow up just like you," they chanted. "Someday when
you're old and grey, you'll want us to visit you on
Father's Day," they continued. "You'll say, 'Come
over kids and visit me,' but we'll say, 'Sorry, Dad,
we're watchin' TV.' Oh, that's OK, Dad, don't be
blue, 'cause we're gonna grow up just like you."

On our way over to the kennels after church, I lec-
tured the children on the absolute rules of conduct for
the rest of the day. They were to go up and play with
the malamute puppy for a few minutes and I would
stay in the car, listening to the baseball game. They
would get all the information on the dog and we would
then go home better informed, in the event that we
ever got serious about owning a dog. I brought out all
the negatives as to why we weren't going to get the
dog. I started with the responsibilities, the problem of
caring for it when we were away from home, the possibility of rabies, the risk of it biting the water softener
man and us getting sued. And I finished with all of the
important issues a prudent family must consider, before making such a costly investment.

At the kennels I couldn't understand what was taking them so long to get the information on the puppy.
Surely the kennel owners had better things to do than
let a gang of children play with their merchandise for
half an hour. As I opened the car door to go up and see

what was keeping the children, a furry ball with four legs came scrambling toward me. He was black with a brown tummy and there was a white diamond on his forehead, between two big brown eyes. I think it was the eyes that did it. He licked my shoes and pulled at my trouser cuffs. He ran around me in circles with his little curved tail wagging so furiously that he looked like an anchored-down helicopter trying to take off. He lay on his back, looking up at me, inviting me to scratch his chest and stomach. He knew who his master was! I said, "Get in the car, Kheemo; let's go home and watch the ball game."

The dog cost five hundred dollars. The fence cost five hundred dollars. He ate the webbing off the patio furniture. He destroyed the flower garden. He chewed up my house slippers and my best jogging shoes. He came right in the house through the screen door, which was locked!

Shortly after his arrival, the kids and I were rough-housing with him in the family room, while my wife was out shopping. Unfortunately, we had selected my wife's favorite Persian rug to romp on and the situation soon got out of hand. As Kheemo and I were doing battle, the dog attacked the rug and sent the fibers flying in all directions.

My wife's Persian masterpiece had a winter scene woven intricately out of different colored threads and textured yarns. In the center was a Canadian snow goose taking flight from a tranquil pond. Evidently malamutes are nearsighted because Kheemo was eating the goose as if it were a gourmet dinner. I grabbed the puppy's jaws and managed to retrieve most of the loose threads before he swallowed them. For the next two hours I tried to weave the loose strings back through the warp and weft threads in the rug in some pattern that would resemble a Canadian snow goose. What I ended up with looked more like a wet turkey!

When my wife returned from the store, the children and I were in the process of straightening the rug and putting our weaving tools away. "What happened to my rug?" she exclaimed, coming closer to examine it. I waved her away. "It's nothing to worry about," I said casually, "the kids and I were chasing around the yard and the house, and we got your Persian rug a little soiled. We shampooed it for you and it would be better for you not to walk on it just yet. Why don't you wait until tomorrow to check it over, after it dries?" I suggested nervously. "It doesn't look right," she said, shaking her head. Before I could stop her she grabbed the vacuum cleaner and sucked the center right out of the rug, where the snow goose had been. "Good heavens," she shrieked, "what have you done to my priceless rug?" I made the weak excuse that it must have been one of those Iranian rugs that don't hold up under normal environmental conditions.

"It was your dog that did this, wasn't it?" my wife said, her voice wavering with emotion. "It wasn't my dog," I argued apologetically, "it was our daughter Dayna's dog that chewed up the rug." "You bought it!" my wife answered coldly. "But she thought it," I countered, proclaiming my innocence.

The temperature was rather cool around the house for the next week or two. Every time my wife walked past the spot where the rug used to lie she muttered things about dogs and husbands as if they belonged together. She also said she wished lecturers would practice what they preached at seminars.

As for Kheemo, he grew up to be a fine family pet and watchdog. Dayna and the rest of the kids believe in their dreams. But they realize how important it is to have someone to help you reach your goals.

The Wheel of Fortune

In order to enlist the support of our associates, family, and friends in achieving our goals, we first must define them. Just by beginning to identify specifically what we want in life, the accomplishment is half done. Most people look at life like a TV game show in which you spin the wheel, try your luck, and win some expensive prizes or go home empty-handed.

I'd like to introduce you to a different kind of "Wheel of Fortune." With this wheel, you can plan ahead to make the odds of winning in your favor from the start. If you understand the basics and follow the steps, you can win by design.

As we begin, let's examine a few relevant terms and definitions:

Luck—*L*aboring *U*nder *C*orrect *K*nowledge. Once we know what we want to do and start preparing and doing it, we begin to have good luck.

Fear—*F*alse *E*ducation *A*ppearing *R*eal. As we learned earlier, most of what we fear is imaginary, has already happened, is easy to solve once defined, or is beyond our control.

Procrastination—Hesitation caused by the fear of results, which can as often be the fear of success as the fear of failure.

Goals—Specific, action-oriented targets that can be defined, discussed, visualized, and committed to writing. Goals should be set just out of your current reach, but not out of sight.

Dreams—Daydreams are goals in the formative stages. Night dreams, normally, are subconscious episodes that help us resolve our emotional conflicts.

Dominant Thoughts—Goals or obsessions that drive your daily life and priorities.

Self-Talk—The silent conversations you have with yourself every minute about your life. Self-talk is also the conversation you have with other people about yourself and your goals.

Rules of the Game—There is only one rule. Your Wheel of Fortune is not a game of chance. It is a game of choice. You will spend your life by the choices you make. There are no timeouts, no substitutions, and the clock is always running.

Warm-up Exercises—Before we spin the wheel for real, let's get our brains limbered up with a few mind-stretching exercises. Answer "yes" or "no" to the following questions:

_____Do I complete the projects I begin?
_____Do I rehearse my goals in my imagination?
_____Do I have a number of bad habits I can't seem to break?
_____Do I have the same daydreams over and over about my success in a given field?
_____Do I usually talk and think about my goals in a positive way?
_____Do I know where I'm going in my life?

Next, let's use our imaginations to think of something enjoyable we want to do. If your dreams came true, what would your life be like? Dream a little by completing these sentences:

One goal I really want is_____
If I had a great deal of money I would_____
I would like to be the kind of person who_____
A place I would like to visit is_____
My life would be better if_____
If I had the time I would_____
If I could start over I would_____

As the final warm-up exercise, honestly consider the major roadblocks that have been holding you back in rolling your Wheel of Fortune down the road of life with greater speed and to more destinations. The following are various obstacles people say prevent them most from getting what they want out of life. Check the ones you feel have restricted or limited you:

___insufficient education

___insufficient capital

___bad economic times

___inflation

___the government

___uncooperative spouse

___negative family upbringing

___chose the wrong profession

___too many dependents

___physically not attractive enough

___discrimination due to sex, race, etc.

___company promotion policies

___in with the wrong crowd

___Viet Nam veteran

___bad credit rating

___wrong political party in power

___alcohol, drugs, etc.

___wrong horoscope

___out of step with the times

___always pick the wrong job

___unresponsive boss

___limited family support

___economically depressed city

___chose obsolete industry

Remember, earlier in this chapter, when I said that you and I are different from most people? I really meant that. I believe that you would not be this far into this book if you were not a winning individual. People with low self-esteem, who are poorly motivated, rarely—if ever—read books that are designed to help them. They concentrate strictly on "escape" pastimes. This book is a journey to discover self, rather than escape from self. The reason I mention this is that I doubt that you checked a large number of items under the major roadblocks that have prevented you from reaching your goals in life.

I think you and I can be honest with ourselves. Perhaps you did not get the education you wanted. Your organization may not recognize your outstanding abilities. Your spouse's primary objective seems to be keeping you humble. Whatever the problem, you and I know that you are responsible for the eventual outcome of your life. You have been given the greatest power in the world—the power to choose. You understand that the goals and decisions you have chosen in the past have brought you to your present circumstances. You also realize that your future will be determined, in large measure, by the goals you have set for yourself that guide your daily decisions. You and I both know that our self-esteem, creative imagination, and feeling of responsibility for causing our own effects are the major roadblocks or green lights on our roads of life. Let's keep these ideas in mind as we consider how to play the Wheel of Fortune.

Looking at the Wheel of Fortune illustration, there are eight segments in the Wheel. For each of the eight segments, I have listed a few goal-starter ideas from which you can begin to construct your own Wheel of Fortune. I know that you may be way ahead of this fundamental approach to goal setting, but even if you are, play along with me as a means of checking your own progress.

Select *one* of the starter ideas I have listed for each of the eight segments, or pick a specific idea that you have been working on. Select something you are going to accomplish by the end of this year and set yourself a deadline for completing it.

GOAL STARTER IDEAS

Select one of the ideas below or list one of your own:

PHYSICAL	Example:
Sports Skill	I'm going to weigh 165 pounds (male)
Different Weight	I'm going to weigh 120 pounds (female)
Eating Right	When? By December 1st
Exercise Schedule	

FAMILY	Example:
Relationship Spouse	Call my mother more often
Relationship Parents	When? Now and twice a month hereafter.

THE WHEEL OF FORTUNE

Relationship Other
  Relatives
New Family Activity

FINANCIAL
Retirement Savings   _____
Property or Securities   When? _____
  Investment
Business Capital
Education Fund

PROFESSIONAL
Continuing Skills
   Education
Higher Pay Scale
Management Promotion
Professional Society
   or License

When? _____

COMMUNITY SUPPORT
Service Organizations
Volunteer Work
Civic Office or
   Committees
Walk- or Bike-a-thons

When? _____

MENTAL
Read Nonfiction
   Literature & Books
Self-improvement
   Courses
Improve Vocabulary
Own Personal Computer

When? _____

SOCIAL
Make New Friends
Dress & Look Your
   Best
Club Activities
New Recreational
   Pursuits

When? _____

SPIRITUAL
Attend Regular
   Religious Services
Read Religious
   Publications
More Time in Meditation
   & Prayer
More Effort Loving
   & Serving Others

When? _____

How to Mine Your "Goal Mind"

Now that you have selected eight goal starters from the Wheel of Fortune, it is time to pick up where most seminars leave off. Remember at the beginning of this chapter when we learned that the reason most people fail to achieve their goals in life is that they never set them in the first place? I am convinced this next step is extremely important in internalizing even the most basic of your goals.

I have a friend and business associate in Denver, Colorado—Mike Mullinnix—who has coauthored and developed with me a specialized goal-setting workshop titled "The Goal Mind." The program is being taught throughout the United States and the free world as an independent seminar and also as a follow-up workshop for my "Psychology of Winning" video seminars. After dealing with several thousand seminar students, Mike and I have discovered that the construction of a specific self-imaging or "self-talk" statement concerning each major goal is a significant step in the goal achievement process.

By reading these "self-talk" statements several times daily or listening to the goal statements as recorded by your own voice, as if you had already achieved them, you can accelerate the internalization of your goals. Your self-image cannot distinguish between reality and something vividly imagined. The habit of repeatedly reinforcing your own goals as if they were in the present tense introduces visual, emotional, and verbal suggestions to your creative imagination at the subconscious level. These suggestions, if repeated in a relaxed environment with frequency, will tend to override your previous habit patterns with a new game plan that you have designed for success.

To steer your Wheel of Fortune down a yellow brick road and convert your "goal mind" into a "gold mine," take the eight goal starters that you selected in each category and define them, specifically, in one sentence.

Example

1. My Physical Goal   <u>is to weigh 165 pounds</u>
   <u>and tone up my muscles</u>
   When? By December 1

2. My Family Goal   _____

   _____

   When? _____

3. My Financial Goal_____

   _____

   When? _____

4. My Professional Goal_____

   _____

   When? _____

5. My Community Support Goal_____

   _____

   When? _____

6. My Mental Goal   _____

   _____

   When? _____

7. My Social Goal   _____

   _____

   When? _____

8. My Spiritual Goal _____

   _____

   When? _____

It is not unusual for successful individuals to be working on four or five goals in each of the eight categories, at the same time. I know many top managers and leaders in every field who review several goal cards each day and listen to audio cassette recordings in their own voice of those goals, on their way to and from their place of business every day. Interestingly enough, these same individuals seem to be the happiest, best adjusted, best married, best parents, and most financially secure people I have ever met. They know where they want to go in life and they are on the right road.

Now that you have one goal in each of the eight categories defined as to what it is and when you plan to accomplish it, get yourself a pack of lined 3 × 5 cards. *Write each of the eight goals on a separate card, as if it has already been reached:*

- Use the pronoun "I" and
- Present tense verbs (am enjoying, am doing, earning, etc.)
- Action modifiers (easily, regularly)
- Emotion words (enthusiastically, happily)
- Goal (present tense)

Examples:

Physical Goal—"I enjoy weighing 120 pounds
(female)   and looking slim in my new
                        bathing suit."
Physical Goal—"I weigh a trim, athletic 165
(male)   pounds and enjoy exercising
                        every day."

As you write these "self-talk" goal statements on the 3 × 5 cards, you should use some subtle refinements in the sentence construction; this can spell the difference between success and failure in your internalization of the goal suggestions. In working with astronauts, Olympic athletes, and clinical psychologists engaged in behavior modification, I have found the following principles to work best for positive self-statements:

1. Always use personal pronouns. Words such as "I," "my," "mine" and "me," will personalize your statements and make them easier to affirm and assimilate.
   Ineffective: "Jogging is good exercise."
   Effective: "I enjoy jogging three miles every day."

2. Keep your self-talk in the present tense. Referring to the past or future dilutes the impact of, or may be counterproductive to, the internalization of your goals.
   Ineffective: "Someday I'll go to Hawaii."
   Effective: "I love the surf and sand in Maui."

3. Keep your goal statements short and concise (four to five seconds long).
   Ineffective: "Now that I have saved five thousand dollars, I may go into business for myself and I hope to succeed."
   Effective: "My business is properly capitalized with the five thousand dollars I put in it."

4. Direct your self-talk toward what you desire, instead of trying to come away from what you don't want. Your mind can't concentrate on the reverse of an idea. If you try to tell yourself not to repeat mistakes, your mind will reinforce the mistake. You want to focus your current dominant thought on your desires, not your dislikes.
   Ineffective: "I can quit smoking."
   "I will lose twenty pounds."
   "I am not late any more."
   "I don't yell at the children."
   "I won't fumble the football."
   Effective: "I am in control of my habits."
   "I weigh a slim, trim 125 pounds."

"I arrive early for appointments."
"I am patient and loving with my kids."
"I guard and control the football."

5. Keep your self-talk noncompetitive, rather than comparing yourself with others.
   Ineffective: "I will become a starter on the team before he or she does."
   Effective: "I am starting on the team and doing the job well."

6. In writing your statements, strive for improvement over your current status. Don't strive for perfection.
   Ineffective: "I'm the best sales executive in the company, making the most money."
   Effective: "I'm doing my best this year, producing twenty percent more than last year."

Once you have correctly written a goal statement on cards for each of the eight categories in the Wheel of Fortune, get in the habit of carrying them on your person everywhere you go, every day. Read the statements in the morning at the beginning of your normal routine, look them over during the day, and read them again before you retire at night. Visualize yourself having already reached each goal. Allow yourself to actually feel the pride of doing well. If possible, record the goals in your own voice on an audio cassette tape, as we suggested in the chapter on The Seed of Creativity.

The Awesome Power of Suggestion

I'm impressed with the methods used by the Soviet Union, East Germany, and Bulgaria in training their Olympic athletes to gain high performance through suggestopedic learning. They instruct an athlete to listen to classical music while at the same time a goal tape, recorded in the athlete's own voice, is softly playing. The individual enjoys and focuses on the music; the goal statements become a subliminal, background sound. The goals, however, should be audible and recognizable.

The rhythmic beat of the slow classical music appears to provide a relaxation mode for the brain, making it most susceptible to visual and audio suggestion and releasing the dominance of the left hemisphere to allow the right hemisphere to respond to the goal affirmations. Since the right hemisphere seems to house most of our negative, subconscious feelings about ourselves, our repeated goal statements may literally change the way we view ourselves and thus alter the direction of our lives.

Don't let the technique of affirmation and simulation give you the false impression that we are brainwashing ourselves or lying to ourselves. What I am suggesting is the opposite from brainwashing, or kidding ourselves. We are, unwittingly, being brainwashed and lied to every day of the week, day and night. The programs we watch, the magazines we read, the inputs we listen to, the people we talk to—all of these are giving us a sensationalized, dramatized perception of what is happening in the world. I perceive most of society's inputs as negative. Isn't it time that you and I concentrated on information designed for our success, rather than our frustration? Isn't it time we switched from washing our minds with "soaps" to programming our minds with goals?

The mind is goal-seeking by design. Successful individuals have game plans and purposes that are clearly defined and to which they constantly refer. They know where they are going every day, every month, and every year. Things don't just happen in their lives. They make life happen for themselves and their loved ones. They know the difference between goal-achieving actions, and activities that are just tension-relieving.

Purpose is the engine that powers our lives. Everyone has purpose. For some it is to eat; for others it is to get through the day. For most Americans it is to make it to Friday so they can celebrate "TGIF" at the local watering hole. For you and me personal growth, contribution, creative expression, loving relationships and spiritual harmony are the common goals that make us try to be uncommon people. Specific, written goals are the tools which make purpose achievable. Since the mind is a biocomputer, it needs definitive instructions and directions. The reason most people don't reach their goals is that they don't define them, learn about them, or ever seriously consider them as believable or achievable.

While the others watch in the viewing audience, you and I will grab our Wheel of Fortune and take command. We can tell the others where we are going, approximately how long it will take, why we are going, what we plan to do along the way, and who will be sharing the adventure with us. You and I live our lives—on purpose!

Ten Action Steps toward Your Goals

1. Set short-range goals that build toward your long-range purpose. It is much more effective to establish goals for the month, six months, or one year, than to project too far into the future. Specific time limits are important measuring devices.

2. Set goals that are just out of reach, but not out of sight. It is critically important to use an incremental approach to success. By setting lower level goals—ones that are relatively easy to accomplish—it is easier to make corrections when you get off target. The achievement of step-by-step goals also builds your confidence.

3. Get group reinforcement by surrounding yourself with motivated individuals interested in the same achievement. Also, review your goals with experts. Get counsel from people with proven track records of success.

4. Establish a reward or ceremony in advance, so that you will have something specific to celebrate upon the accomplishment of each of your goals. It may be a trip, a family dinner, some special recreation, new clothing, or personal item.

5. Try a different kind of New Year's celebration. Put your goals for this year in an envelope. Encourage your family members to do the same. On New Year's Eve or New Year's Day, open the envelopes and see how well you did in accomplishing what you set out to do. It is a fantastic way to end another great year. Then set your goals for the new year (before all the postseason football games dominate your attention).

6. Use a desk top or briefcase calendar to set your goals for next month. What will you do, where will you go, and with whom will you communicate?

7. Use a pocket, week-at-a-glance calendar to set your activities for next week that will take you step-by-step toward your monthly and annual goals.

8. Use an 8½ × 11 lined folio pad to set the most important goals of all—your daily priorities. At the close of each day set your priorities for tomorrow. Review your list at the beginning of each new day, before you make your first call or appointment. Check off each item as it is accomplished and carry over those priorities not completed, into the following day's agenda.

9. Don't share your goals with negative people or cynics. Share your goals with people who really

care about you and want to help you. And make certain you take the advice of winners. Remember, misery loves company. Some people would just as soon you stayed in the same rut along with them!

10. Don't depend upon the government for your long-range financial security. Pay yourself each month, by putting a sum of money in a savings account for your future, as if you were paying your house payment. You are your best Social Security.

Questions about Your Purpose

1. What is one of your personal goals this month? What will you do today that contributes to that goal?

2. What is one of your professional goals this month? Have you shared this goal with anyone who can reinforce your purpose?

3. Do you have a game plan for the year?

4. Do you have physical fitness goals established? Check to see that they are stated in specific language.

5. Will you be able to live in later years without worrying about Social Security? Have you decided how much you will put away in savings each month?

6. What are you going to do tomorrow? Will you carry over the items that you didn't get to today, and make them tomorrow's goals?

6 | The Seed of Communication

REACH OUT AND TOUCH SOMEONE
- Walking in Another's Moccasins
- Getting on Their Wavelength
- Love Letters to Live By
- The Sixth Best-Kept Secret of Total Success
- Take Time to Listen
- Communication Is from Inside to Outside
- The Way to Climb Up from "Never"
- The Power of One-on-One
- Ten Action Steps to Better Communication

The libraries and bookstores are filled with volumes of material on effective communication. I have decided to concentrate on two basic aspects of communication that I believe are the most important: empathy and love.

I came to understand the meaning of empathy at a PACE seminar in Carefree, Arizona. The PACE program—which stands for Personal And Company Effectiveness—has an excellent reputation in teaching self-awareness to executives and to married couples.

Jim Newman, founder of the program, was our instructor for the four-day seminar. He has a special gift for using true-life incidents to explain profound truths. As we discussed how communication and our relationships with others is one of the critical keys to happiness, Jim told a story about a lady who had attended one of his previous retreats.

Walking in Another's Moccasins

The lady had taken her five-year-old son shopping at a large department store during the Christmas season. She knew it would be fun for him to see all the decorations, window displays, toys, and Santa Claus. As she dragged him by the hand, twice as fast as his little legs could move, he began to fuss and cry, clinging to his mother's coat. "Good heavens, what on earth is the matter with you?" she scolded, impatiently. "I brought you with me to get in the Christmas spirit. Santa doesn't bring toys to little crybabies!"

His fussing continued as she tried to find some bargains during the last-minute rush on December 23. "I'm not going to take you shopping with me, ever again, if you don't stop that whimpering," she admonished. "Oh well, maybe it's because your shoes are untied and you are tripping over your own laces," she said, kneeling down in the aisle to tie his shoes.

As she knelt down beside him, she happened to look up. For the first time, she viewed a large department store through the eyes of her five-year-old. From that position there were no baubles, bangles, beads, presents, gaily decorated display tables, or animated toys. All that could be seen was a maze of corridors too high to see above, full of giant, stovepipe legs and huge posteriors. These mountainous strangers, with feet as big as skateboards, were pushing and shoving, bumping and thumping, rushing and crushing. Rather than fun, the scene looked absolutely terrifying! She elected to take her child home and vowed to herself never to impose her version of a good time on him again.

On their way out of the store, the mother noticed Santa Claus seated in a pavilion decorated like the North Pole. She knew that letting her little boy meet Santa Claus in person would go a long way toward his remembering the Christmas shopping disaster as a pleasant, rather than unpleasant, experience.

"Go stand in line with the other children, and sit up on Santa's lap," she coaxed. "Tell him what you want for Christmas, and smile while you're talking so I can take your picture for the family album."

Even though a Santa Claus was standing outside the store entrance ringing a bell, and although they had seen another Santa at the previous shopping center, the five-year-old was pushed forward to enjoy a personal chat with the "real one."

When the strange-looking man with the beard, glasses, and red suit stuffed with pillows hoisted the boy up onto his lap, he laughed loudly (which he felt was important to the role) and tickled the little boy in the ribs.

"And what would you like for Christmas, son?" Santa boomed jovially.

"I'd like to get down," the boy replied softly.

Santa Claus was a stranger to the little boy. This youngster was confused by seeing two other Santas before his mother had asked him to get up on the "real" one's lap. It isn't fun for a five-year-old to do last-minute shopping in a crowded mall jammed with impatient adults. By kneeling down and tying her son's shoe, and by considering his uneasiness with a strange Santa Claus, the mother was experiencing a rare lesson in empathy that too few of us ever share with those we care about most.

Newman's story about the little boy caused all of us at the seminar to stop and think about our own communications with others. As he was closing the session, he passed out bookmarks with the old Sioux Indian prayer printed on it. I still have mine and it becomes more precious as the years go by. It reads: "Oh Great Spirit, grant me the wisdom to walk in another's moccasins before I criticize or pass judgment."

In small group discussions after Jim Newman's lecture, we agreed that in communication there is nothing as important as "walking in another's moccasins" before you speak your mind. Empathy is one of the keys to communication. It is "feeling with" the other person. More than sympathy, or "feeling for" an individual, empathy is the process of trying to understand the other person's point of view, as if you were that person. Empathy is when you watch the marathon runners at the 20-mile mark, and your own legs ache. Empathy is watching a rerun of one of the *Rocky* movies and hardly being able to lift your arms at the end of round fifteen.

The seminar broke on a high note, and most of the participants left the meeting feeling as if they could be champions like Rocky in their own personal and professional arenas. It had a different effect on me. I went for a walk in the desert twilight to think about what I had learned. The tall saguaro cactus trees, like silent strangers, cast mute shadows on the sand. As I strolled among them I wondered if any of my family or associates looked at me as if I were somewhat removed and aloof, like the cactus.

I wondered how empathic I really was. I asked myself some questions and tried to visualize the answers. *How would I like a parent like me, if I were my children? How would I like to be married to me? How would I like a manager like me?* These were difficult questions.

Do I only give lip service to being a good communicator? I queried myself. *Do I take my relationships for granted or do I truly know what the others in my life are feeling, needing, wanting, and saying?*

I couldn't honestly answer yes to all of the questions. I knew that I could improve in the way I "feel with" and "feel for" the individuals in my life. As I returned to my room, I decided to switch on my receiver and really listen to what people are trying to say.

Getting on Their Wavelength

One of the best ways to begin to practice empathy is to be more open and sensitive to the needs and differences of others. Successful individuals look at relative viewpoints rather than absolutes. The prelude to empathy is realizing that each human being on earth is a person with equal rights to fulfill his or her own potential in life. It is understanding that skin color, birthplace, political beliefs, sex, financial status, and intelligence are not measures of worth or worthiness. The path to communication is accepting the fact that every human being is a distinctly unique individual—and thinking how good that is. No two people are alike, not even identical twins.

We are unique in our fingerprints, our footprints, and even in our voiceprints! AT&T, knowing that each of us speaks with a sound frequency unmatched by any other person, is developing a "Voice-print" system that will provide instant, positive identification, electronically. By stating your name audibly into a microphone at the store counter or bank window, your own "Voice-print" frequency will be compared with the one on file at a central computer. This process will do away with bad checks and stolen credit cards. Even the best impersonator can't fake another person's voice frequency.

We speak at different frequencies and think at different frequencies. Often we hear people say: "We're not on the same wavelength." Human beings have been trying to get on the same wavelength with each other for many centuries. It is little wonder that there is so much discord in family, social, and international life.

Everyone hears a different drummer, sees through a different lens, and perceives through a different filter. Your decisions are a result of a unique computer read-out system in your brain.

Empathy is understanding that a busload of people riding home from work through the city will see the same scene from entirely different viewpoints. One will see the depressing, dilapidated buildings. Another will see an ideal sight for a redevelopment project. Another, his face buried in his own problems, will see nothing. Still another person, her eyes eagerly scanning a textbook, will see a way out of the ghetto.

It is important to try to view the world of others as they see it—rather than as we see it. One way to do this is to look for the good in others, regardless how different their appearance, their life-style, and their particular beliefs are from our own. By looking for the good in others, you are communicating love. Love is the one message we all need most.

Love Letters to Live By

Valentines are love letters with simple statements of affection. I would like to give you a valentine to explain as fundamentally as possible what love really is.

One basic definition of love, as a verb, is "to value." Love should be a verb, not a noun or adverb. Love is an active emotion. It is not static. Love is one of the few experiences in life that we can best keep by giving it away. Love is the act of demonstrating value for and looking for the good in another person.

> L—is for Listen. To love someone is to listen unconditionally to his values and needs without prejudice.

> O—is for Overlook. To love someone is to overlook the flaws and the faults in favor of looking for the good.

V—is for Voice. To love someone is to voice your approval of him on a regular basis. There is no substitute for honest encouragement, positive "strokes" and praise.

E—is for Effort. To love someone is to make a constant effort to spend the time, to make the sacrifice, to go the extra mile to show your interest.

In an earlier chapter on self-esteem, we talked about the need to love yourself before you can give that love away. Loving requires independence and is based upon the ability to share ourselves with others out of choice, not out of dependent need. True love is that relationship formed by two individuals who have the ability of separately sustaining themselves. Only independent people are free to choose to stay in a relationship. People who are dependent remain in a relationship out of necessity.

Because we have become a more dependent, narcissistic society motivated by the desire for immediate gratification, many people are less able to express themselves in spontaneous, intimate communication. Although they have become skilled technicians of the sexual act, they are afraid to expose themselves to the vulnerability inherent in intimacy. In spite of the fact that sexual information is abundant, the quality of sexual behavior is not much improved. Our intimate relationships may even be suffering under the slick media-hype which promotes performance over closeness and commitment. While sex is everywhere, intimacy seems to have all but disappeared. Ironically enough, the secret to intimacy is not hard to learn at all.

The Sixth Best-Kept Secret of Total Success

I love my wife. I love the thought and act of being with her; but I'm not dependent upon her. She loves me, too, and I know she doesn't need me for her security. She was independent before we met and she is independent now. We are two independent persons, sharing our values and caring for each other.

When I am with her, time is like a thief who quickly steals our precious moments. When we are apart, the hours pass by as if time were but an endless desert, with no other side. Most of all, my wife is like a rare flower. She wilts softly when she is passed by—unseen, unnoticed, or untouched. She blossoms brightly and fragrantly when she is cared for and nourished.

I love to touch my wife. I also love to touch our kids and hold them. That may sound silly since they range in age from 26 to 11. We have four beautiful girls, with two boys in the middle (both of whom are bigger than me). I hope I never get away from my compulsive habit of touching my family. I have made my share of mistakes in rearing our children, but I should get pretty good marks in the loving department.

In my lifetime, I've read many books on love, the art of loving, and the ability to love. I do not believe I could quote from any of them a better definition than "a touch is worth a thousand words." One of the most heartwarming scenes I can remember is a couple, celebrating their golden wedding anniversary, holding hands under the table while the waiters and waitresses were singing "Happy Anniversary to You!"

There are no rules of etiquette for keeping in touch with those you really care for; however, here are some ideas which have been valuable to me:

- Not a morning should go by but that the opening minutes are devoted to mutually satisfying words and actions. The first words I speak to Susan each morning of my life are, "Good morning. I love you."

- After the day's activities are completed, and as the family or couple re-convenes,

devote the first few minutes of greeting totally to the other person. Never greet anyone with a pressing question or a complaint. Don't forget to touch. Relax soon
after you arrive home. Surprise your mate
with a card, a remembrance, or what my
wife and I call a "Happy." Pretend you are
still dating. Always look forward to seeing
your loved ones. If you really want to be
loved in life, you must first be loveable.
There is no such thing as love on demand,
or "You promised me ten years ago you
would always love me!" Love is a daily,
mutual exchange of value.

- The last words I speak each night are,
  "Good night, I love you."

- Nothing transmits value so clearly as the
  physical touch. Use your sense of touch
  generously.

**The Sixth Best-Kept Secret of Total Success is
that a touch is worth a thousand words.**

Touch is the magic wand of intimacy. Love is keeping in touch.

Take Time to Listen

Intimacy, touching, communicating, all take time. The
most precious moments you and I ever spend with our
children are those moments just before they go to
sleep at night. Many activities are going on in the normal family in the early evening. There is dinner,
homework, chores, video games, finances, meetings,
television, phone calls, visitors, friends and pets, just
to name a few. Little wonder that the average Ameri-

can parents spend less than seven minutes each week alone with each child, one-on-one, at a time when each one is receptive. Children spend more time watching television than they do communicating with their parents or acquiring an education. Our relationship with our children has been referred to as "The Seven-Minutes-Per-Week Syndrome."

On one of my speaking tours a few years ago, my wife and I were discussing our need to spend more time with our children. We agreed that we would make an effort to do something personally and separately with each of the children once each month, in addition to group outings. We already had instituted the practice of taking them to a different ethnic restaurant for dinner each month for the cultural experience. We both understood the need simply to be with our children, to listen to them. What our kids didn't need from us was more advice or counsel. They certainly didn't need to attend another "Psychology of Winning" seminar given by their father. Each of them could give the program from memory as it was. As we were flying home from New York, my wife began to write a poem to remind us of what we had promised each other about our communication goals with our children. I finished the poem before we landed in San Diego:

Take a Moment to Listen

Take a moment to listen today
   To what your children are trying to say;
Listen today, whatever you do
   Or they won't be there to listen to you.

Listen to their problems, listen for their
   needs,
   Praise their smallest triumphs, praise their
     smallest deeds;
Tolerate their chatter, amplify their laughter,
   Find out what's the matter, find out what
     they're after.

But tell them that you love them, every
    single night
  And though you scold them, be sure you
    hold them;
Tell them "Everything's all right;
    tomorrow's looking bright!"

Take a moment to listen today
  To what your children are trying to say;
Listen today, whatever you do
  And they will come back to listen to you.

That poem holds truths and principles that I've learned the hard way. I haven't always been a great listener. I haven't always taken enough time to listen to my children and to experience their world from their vantage point. When my children were young, I was busy trying to climb to the top of the success heap. I had not yet learned what the real meaning of success was all about.

I used to listen to my children with "half an ear." I was preoccupied with business or my own goals, and I feigned full attention. The only person I fooled was myself. I also had the habit of communicating with my children and my wife by playing the game of "Can You Top This?" Whenever they would tell me something really exciting about their world, or something that one of their friends or a friend's parents had done, I could hardly wait until they finished telling me so that I could outdo them with my own fantastic experience. Sometimes when my kids or my wife would admit that they had done something stupid or made a mistake, I responded with an "I told you so." They admitted their vulnerability and I scolded them for it, which made them hesitant to open up in the future.

Today, I don't play those "Can You Top This?" games anymore. Those games are not for the family or for any other relationships for that matter. And yet we hear these games being played every day in every business office and institution in the world. In many ways, the way we communicate in adult life is the result of how we were raised. Our ability, or the lack of it, to communicate is the result of our family environment and it all began when we were infants. Our parents either nurtured us with love or passed along their hang-ups.

Communication Is from Inside to Outside

No matter how we try to mask or disguise our feelings by playing "Can You Top This?" communication games, we aren't fooling anyone. No matter how confident or sure of ourselves we try to appear, we still project on the outside how we feel about ourselves on the inside. For example, when we aren't feeling well physically, we don't look well at the skin or surface level. Correspondingly, when we don't feel good about ourselves emotionally or mentally, we don't seem to make a very good impression with our looks, personal grooming, and conversation.

A first step in good communications is a good appearance. It is the way to gain the attention of people who are important to us long enough to project our inside value, like a good book among the thousands available on the bookstore shelf.

As good communicators, you and I get in touch with strangers by extending our hands first, knowing it is the time-proven courtesy for paying value to others. Along with a firm handshake, we use direct eye contact and a warm, open smile to project our interest in communication. We volunteer our own name first when meeting strangers, and we precede our name with "Good morning," "Good afternoon," or "Good evening." This also holds true for telephone communication.

Once you and I introduce ourselves we become active listeners who listen for feelings with empathy. We understand that listeners learn a great deal, while talkers learn nothing.

We look forward to new contacts and friends. We talk easily with strangers. We look at people when talking to them or listening to them. We listen openly and carefully, even though we may disagree with what they are saying.

We treat the other person as an equal. We listen to the seemingly dull and ignorant because they, too, have their story.

We ask questions without imposing. We try to find special qualities in strangers and praise them sincerely. We draw strangers out by getting them to talk about themselves.

We are easy to understand and easy to get along with. We don't assume what the other party's reaction will be to what we say, nor do we try to read his or her mind.

We are confident in meeting strangers because we understand that, no matter how secure other people may seem, almost everyone is eager to meet new people to gain a friendship or for personal development. We realize that almost everyone has a normal tendency to harbor a little fear of rejection or of exploitation.

When you and I face a potential friend, business prospect, or one of our own family members, our attitude is service-oriented, not self-oriented. Our concern is for the other person, not ourselves. When we have others' interests at heart, not just our own, they can sense it. They may not be able to put into words why they feel that way, but they do. Conversely, people get an uneasy feeling when they talk with people who have only their own self-interests in mind. It's the manifestation of nonverbal communication: "What you are speaks so loudly, I can't hear what you are saying."

The tongue can lie, but the body acts instinctively, subconsciously, and honestly. We learned in Chapter 2 that while the left hemispheres of our brains are conducting the verbal process in communicating, our right hemispheres are both sending and observing facial expressions, body language, voice inflections and other subconscious "feelings." People telegraph their intentions and feelings without even realizing what is happening. For that reason, you and I watch and listen to the "whole person."

Successful communicators know that all of us hear and see differently. Since we tend to get back from people what we give them, it is best to project ourselves with simple, constructive, supportive ideas. If we want to be loved, we need to communicate in positive, "loveable" language.

The following are a few words you should either delete from or add to the vocabulary of your daily communications. Please get rid of the words in the left-hand column and substitute the corresponding words in the right-hand column:

Words to Forget	Words to Remember
I can't	I can
I'll try	I will
I have to	I want to
should have	will do
could have	my goal
someday	today
if only	next time
Yes, but	I understand
problem	opportunity
difficult	challenging
stressed	motivated
worried	interested
impossible	possible
I, me, my	You, your
hate	love

The Way to Climb Up from "Never"

One of the most constructive, loveable men I know is Joe Sorrentino. We met in a hotel coffee shop after a productivity program in which we had both participated as keynote speakers. He had been the first speaker, and I the last. He was the toughest act I have ever had to follow, because his act was straight from the soul.

He shouldn't have been such a formidable platform personality—not with his early track record! In fact, he really shouldn't have been the keynote speaker for a "Fortune 500" company, based upon the first twenty years of his life. His early career looked more like something out of *Who's He?* rather than *Who's Who.*

The son of a Brooklyn sanitation worker, he grew up in a neighborhood where it was only safe to go for a walk when the policemen were having their annual parade—and you were marching in it! He became a teenage gang leader and served time in a New York reform school. To get straightened out, he joined the Marine Corps and ended up in a Parris Island padded cell for the delinquent and incorrigible, before he was summarily discharged.

As Joe and I talked about his life, I wondered how he'd ever turned his life around. His neighborhood environment and his home environment weren't exactly what you would call ideal for building high self-esteem. His dad had expressed a theory to him that children "grow up good or bad themselves—it's what they're made of inside that counts." Joe also said that in addition to wondering whether he had been "born to lose" (because of his dad's theory), there was something else he had to contend with. His dad always drew a comparison between his older brother and him: "Your brother never gets into trouble," he would say, "and I don't have to yell at him." Between these early inputs and the pressure of the neighborhood peer group, you can see that Joe wasn't exactly nurtured with Seeds of Greatness.

Amazingly, in spite of all the "weeds" in his early nurturing, Joe Sorrentino is one of the most successful, sensitive human beings I have ever met. He feels that his parents, overall, had a positive effect on his life. He remembers their moments of understanding as much as he does the days and nights of sweltering frustration. He also vividly recalls "the influence of a caring teacher, a concerned priest, and a bowling alley owner."

Joe Sorrentino has told of his incredible evolution from loser to winner in several powerful books. One of his works, *Up From Never,* won a notable book award from the American Library Association. In one of his more recent books, *The Concrete Cradle,* Sorrentino gives credit for his turnaround to the people in his life who cared for him on a one-on-one basis:

> For a long time I had been a hopeless student, until I met Miss Lawsen, my seventh grade teacher. As a result of her concern and confidence, I applied myself to learning and eventually achieved the highest grade average in junior high school. Regrettably, peer pressure in high school tipped my inner balance back to destructiveness and street violence—fighting every week, failing all my subjects until I was finally expelled at the end of my freshman year. But when I returned to night high school at the age of twenty, I had the memory of Miss Lawsen and the academic aptitude she had nurtured in me.[1]

Joe Sorrentino, disgraced throughout his youth, radically changed his life with the realization that his only chance for survival was through education. After graduating from high school he went on to the University of California where he graduated magna cum laude. To clear his bad military record, Sorrentino reenlisted in the Marine Corps and became the first

---

1. Sorrentino, Joseph N., *The Concrete Cradle* (Los Angeles: Wollstonecraft, Inc., 1975), p. 184.

person in history ever to receive an honorable discharge, after having been previously discharged under less than honorable conditions.

In 1967, Sorrentino was graduated as a top student leader from Harvard Law School. Today he is an outstanding juvenile court judge in Los Angeles, teaches law, and lectures at the University of Southern California. He is also one of the most sought-after speakers in America for his message on self-determination and how to combat the social ills in our country.

What he has learned, one-on-one, from Miss Lawsen and a handful of others has given him the courage and incentive to alter his destiny. Now he is devoting his life to the one-on-one nurturing of his own family and the hundreds of young people who enter his courtroom every year, looking for a ray of light in the darkness.

The Power of One-on-One

Examples of the power of one-on-one communication are everywhere.

Frank Sinatra learned his superb breath control in singing from his band leader, Tommy Dorsey. Helen Keller became a person because of Anne Sullivan. Plato learned from Socrates. Jesse Owens credits his winning of the long jump in the 1936 Olympics to a tip given him by his top German competitor, Luz Long. In the middle of the competition, after Owens had already fouled twice on takeoff, Long gave Owens a helpful hint on how to correct his takeoff point. The result was a record-breaking leap of over twenty-six feet which stood more than twenty years.

Artists have always learned more from observing other artists than from going to classes or observing nature. You and I are master artists who have the opportunity to breathe new colors, shading, and perspective into the lives of other artists who are struggling with their oils, brushes, and canvases. Think back to the people who have had the most influence on you. You will likely find that they have been people who really cared about you—your parents, a fine teacher, a business associate, a good friend—someone who was interested in you. The only people you will influence to any great degree will be the people you care about. When you are with people you care about, *their* interest—rather than your own—will be uppermost in your mind.

Our success in getting along with others and communicating effectively with them depends solely upon our ability to recognize their needs and help them fill those needs. Some people try to force their ideas upon others. You and I use light to show the way.

Remember the Aesop's fable in which the wind and the sun argued over which was the stronger? The wind said, "Do you see that old man down there? I can make him take his coat off quicker than you can."

The sun agreed to go behind a cloud while the wind blew up a storm. However, the harder the wind blew, the firmer the old man wrapped his coat around him.

Eventually the wind gave up and the sun came out from behind the cloud and smiled kindly upon the old man. Before long, the old man mopped his brow, pulled off his coat, and strolled on his way. The sun knew the secret: warmth, friendliness, and a gentle touch are always stronger than force and fury.

Ten Action Steps to Better Communication

1. It is never too late to communicate. Don't wait for fear of what the response might be. Remember Parkinson's latest law: "The vacuum created by a failure to communicate will quickly be filled with rumor, misrepresentation, drivel, and poison."

2. In the communication process, knowledge is not always wisdom; sensitivity is not always accuracy; sympathy is not always understanding. Em-

pathy is never assuming anything until you have "walked a mile in their moccasins."

3. Take full responsibility for success in the communication process. As a listener, take full responsibility for hearing what the others are trying to say. As a talker, take full responsibility for being certain they understand what you are saying. Never meet anyone halfway in your relationships. Always give 100 percent.

4. Look at yourself through other people's eyes. Imagine being your parents. Imagine being that person married to you. Imagine being your child or your employee. When you come into a room or office, what do you think a stranger's first impression will be of you? Why?

5. Listen for truth and speak the truth. Don't let the ads and the fads make you one of the countless victims of greed. When you see or hear something that impresses you, check the validity of the source. Rather than hearing what you want to hear, listen for the facts of the matter. Remember, everything you communicate is your opinion, based upon your impressions from limited sources. Keep expanding your information bank from proven authorities.

6. View everything you hear with open-minded examination. Be open-minded enough to consider it without prejudice, and analytical enough to research and test its integrity.

7. See both the positive and negative sides of the issue, and pursue the positive side.

8. Check to see if you shift "roles" easily and appropriately, from business executive, to courteous driver, to parent, to friend, to confidant, to lover, to teacher.

9. Step back from the canvas of your own life and consider the kind of people who are attracted to you and the kind of people to whom you are attracted. Are they the same type? Do you attract winners? Are you attracted to people who are more or less successful than yourself? Why?

10. Develop that magic "touch." Reach out today, tonight, tomorrow, and every day for the rest of your life. There is a flower waiting to be nurtured and a Joe Sorrentino standing in the shadows.

Questions about Your Communication

1. Do you know how others see you? Are you willing to ask?

2. Do others feel their best around you? What do you do to make them feel good?

3. Do you listen more than you talk? With whom? Everyone? Only certain people?

4. Do you project your best self consistently? Specifically how do you try to do this?

5. Do you look for the good in others with an open mind? List some recent examples.

6. Do you touch the people you love? How often?

7 | The Seed of Faith

THE POWER OF POSITIVE BELIEVING

- **The Seventh Best-Kept Secret of Total Success**
- **Why It's "Snowing" All over America**
- **How Arnold Broke the World's Weight Lifting Record**
- **Getting High (Naturally)!**
- **The Incurable Optimist**
- **Why Lee Trevino Is Always Lucky**
- **Larry's Temporary Inconvenience**
- **"It's Still Me Inside"**
- **Ten Action Steps to Optimism**

When we talk about faith—and belief—we have to refer to the greatest book ever written, and the greatest Teacher of the ages on the subject. He summed it up when He said: "Go thy way; and as thou hast believed, so be it done unto thee."

This simple statement cuts both ways, like a two-edged sword. Faith is the key to unlock the door of success for every human being. Or it is the lock that imprisons and keeps that human being from ever experiencing success.

Dr. Ernest Holmes, who devoted his life to teaching this great truth, explained it another way. "Here is a power which every person has, but which few people use consciously. One individual does not possess this power above another, or to a greater degree. Everyone has it, since everyone lives and has consciousness. The question then is not: Do we have the power? It is merely: Are we using it correctly?"

As a positive power, faith is the promise of the realization of things hoped for and unseen. As a negative power, it is the premonition of our deepest fears and unseen darkness. There is no such thing as the absence of or lack of faith. There is simply the replacement of faith, with its opposite belief—despair.

The Seventh Best-Kept Secret of Total Success

Much has been written through the ages and in recent years concerning the self-fulfilling prophecy. My old friend S. I. Hayakawa refers to the self-fulfilling prophecy as a statement that is neither true, nor false, but is capable of becoming true if it is believed. We learned in the first chapter on creativity and the imagination, that the mind can't distinguish between something that is real and something that is vividly imagined. That is why the concepts of faith and belief are so important.

The Seventh Best-Kept Secret of Total Success is that life is a self-fulfilling prophecy; you won't necessarily get what you want in life, but in the long run you will usually get what you expect.

Science and religion are very closely allied in the implications resulting from studies of the brain during the past ten years. Although we have much to learn in understanding the mechanisms in the brain and central nervous system, we are aware of the inextricable relationship between psyche and soma—mind and body. There is a definite reaction in the body as the result of the thoughts and concerns of the mind. What the mind harbors, the body manifests in some way.

For example, when our fears and worries turn into anxiety, we suffer distress. The distress activates the endocrine system in our bodies and the production of hormones and antibodies changes. Our natural immunity system is less active and our resistance levels are lowered. We become more vulnerable to outside bacteria, virus, and other environmental hazards, which are always present.

In her provocative, solidly founded book, *The Aquarian Conspiracy,* Marilyn Ferguson describes the brain's mastermind or indirect influence on every function of the body: heart rate, immune response, hormones, etc. She says its mechanisms are linked by an alarm network, "and it has a kind of dark genius, organizing disorders appropriate to our most neurotic imaginings."[1] I've always made generalizations that ulcers are not what you eat; they're what's eating you. There is evidence that some forms of asthma are psychosomatic, that they are related more to a smothering relationship such as a doting parent ("smother love") rather than an outside allergen. There have also been cases where hay fever and asthma attacks have been brought on by the patient's seeing pictures of goldenrod or holding a plastic rose.

Ferguson goes on to make the point that when we describe how we feel, we may unwittingly be forecast-

---

1. Ferguson, Marilyn, *The Aquarian Conspiracy* (Los Angeles: Tarcher, Inc., 1980), p. 253.

ing our future. For example, if we say we feel "picked on" or that someone gives us "a pain in the neck," we may literally end up with acne or neck spasms. The strong emotions and loneliness associated with what we call a "broken heart" can lead to heart failure. There is also an apparent link between "bottled-up emotions" and the growth of tumors or other cancers. A "splitting headache" may be precipitated by someone being pulled in opposite directions. And the "rigid personality" has been identified as a factor in some cases of arthritis. What is your daily life-style, routine, and conversation forecasting, as far as your own health is concerned?

Faith is the house of many beliefs. It's time we put the house in order.

Why It's "Snowing" All over America

In Chapter 3 we talked about responsibility and irresponsibility. We indicated that many individuals in our society continue throughout their lives at the same level of emotional immaturity they displayed as adolescents. To understand what's happening in America today, we need to realize the extent to which our young adults have been made excessively dependent on parental support. We have raised our own privileged society, with more and more children rewarded with material goods and payoffs as a consequence of "being there," rather than for their contributions in an openly competitive society. Young adults maturing today, who have been led to believe by their parents and the media that "pain is unacceptable" and "stress can be cured in sixty seconds," have difficulty coping with early challenges and setbacks. They want to find true, loving relationships, but love requires independence and self-esteem. What results is an escape from the type of commitments and sacrifices that are necessary in honest, intimate communications. The escape route is through sexual promiscuity where the only risks are pregnancy and venereal disease—which risks they seem willing to take—and drug abuse, which gets them high unnaturally, without their having to make an effort for the rewarding feeling.

Today, regardless of the season in which you are reading this book, there is a blanket of snow outside. It is snowing everywhere in America. The real name of the "snow" is cocaine.

It is our new "national immediate gratification" status symbol. By conservative estimates, ten million individuals in this country use cocaine regularly, and at least another five million have been experimenting with it. The use of the drug has more than doubled during the past ten years and there is no leveling off in sight. It looks like a long, cold, white winter.

We're not describing a teenage, young adult, or ghetto phenomenon. It is happening in your hometown and mine, in upper- and middle-class America, at every age level. Cocaine advocates say it's the best of both worlds. It gets you high for half an hour or so with a snort and you come down with no cancer, no Monday morning hangover . . . just no-risk fun and games. Well, it doesn't work that way. As you and I have learned, the Law of Cause and Effect is always in force. According to Ronald Siegel, a psychopharmacologist at UCLA, "Extreme cocaine dosages light a kind of fire in the brain." With chronic use, the drug displays aftereffects which can include depression, insomnia, and psychosis. Through repeated "sniffing," it can also cause ulcers inside the nose which can perforate the nasal septum, requiring surgery. Falling from a high may cause such a letdown that the only immediate solution is another snort of cocaine. The vicious circle has begun.

Along with my good friends Art Linkletter and Zig Ziglar, I have learned that it does little good to stand up on the platform and "preach" against the evils of drug abuse. We find that the more bad news you spread, the more it sells. By dignifying the problem with so much ranting and raving about what's wrong in America, we think more harm than good is done. After all, the people who are "doing drugs" are trying to escape from all the bad news in their lives already. More of the same is going to lead to more of the same for them. We need education combined with a positive alternative to their synthetic good times. Certainly, no young adult or teenager is going to listen to members of an older generation who talk down drugs while tilting up their glasses for that good feeling and some real gusto.

How Arnold Broke the World's Weight Lifting Record

It was Saturday, November 1, 1980 and Arnold Lemerand was taking a stroll. He heard some children screaming and hurried over to where they had been playing near a construction site. A massive, cast-iron pipe had become dislodged and had rolled down on top of the children, pinning five-year-old Philip Toth against the earth. The boy's head was being forced into the dirt directly under the huge pipe and certain suffocation appeared to be imminent.

Arnold Lemerand looked around but there was no one to help him in the attempted rescue. He did the only thing he could. He reached down and lifted the 1,800-pound cast-iron pipe off Philip's head. After the incident, he tried again to lift the pipe and could not even budge it. His grown sons tried to move it, but they failed as well.

In an interview later with the Associated Press, Mr. Lemerand, who was 56 at the time, said that he had suffered a major heart attack six years before. "I try to avoid heavy lifting," he smiled, with the young boy's arms around his neck.

We read about such miraculous power surges every so often, don't we? We hear of grandmothers lifting cars and firemen making impossible rescues in burning buildings, exhibiting superhuman strength. Those kinds of stories used to sound rather tall to me, since I've always been a man to check the source and document the advice that people give me as to its validity.

Getting High (Naturally)!

In recent years, I have become a real believer. I don't mean a believer in the sense of a religious faith; I received that faith nearly twenty years ago at ten thousand feet, in the cockpit of a private plane I was flying with Louis Evans, Jr. He was the pastor of our La Jolla Presbyterian Church at the time. More recently, however, I have become a real believer in *the power of faith* and what it can do.

During the middle 1970s I began to learn about how the mind can affect the body and how our thoughts can give us a natural high or make us ill. I was in Sarasota, Florida, serving as president of the International Society for Advanced Education, a nonprofit foundation formed by leading health scientists to study preventive medicine and a holistic approach to wellness. The society was sponsoring continuing medical education seminars in cooperation with the University of Pittsburgh, the University of Nebraska, Johns Hopkins University, Harvard University, and other medical schools.

At some of the seminars, presenters described the research of Dr. Avram Goldstein, director of the Addiction Research Foundation at Stanford University. Dr. Goldstein and his associates had suspected the existence of substances in our brains similar to morphine and heroin. In 1971 they located receptor areas in the brain which act as "locks" that only these unknown substances would fit, like "keys." Along with other researchers, who were working independently in their respective laboratories, Goldstein discovered that our brains contained these "keys" in the form of natural hormones. Several have been identified including enkephalin, endorphin, beta-endorphin, and dynorphin. All of these hormones serve as natural pain relievers many times more powerful than morphine. Beta-endorphin is fifty times more powerful than morphine, and dynorphin is one hundred ninety times more potent than morphine.

Scientists already knew that hormones play an important role in regulating certain of our biological processes. Adrenaline is the hormone that enables us to "fight or flee," in the face of danger or in response to a call for peak physical performance. Insulin regulates the sugar levels in our blood. Now these later discoveries are showing us that morphine-like hormones are being manufactured in our own bodies to block pain and give us a "natural high."

Dr. Roger Guillemin of the Salk Institute in La Jolla, where I used to work, found two of the endorphin hormones and, subsequently, won the Nobel prize in medicine for other work on hormones. In one test, using endorphin supplied by Guillemin, Japanese researchers injected minute amounts of the hormone into fourteen men and women suffering intense pain from cancer. From a single injection, they all felt relief from their pain for one to three days. In another experiment, fourteen expectant mothers were given endorphin during labor. All reported immediate and lasting pain relief and delivered normal babies.

In 1978, a University of California research team made an interesting discovery that seemed to confirm the earlier findings concerning endorphins. You are familiar with the "placebo effect" (*placebo* literally means "I shall please"). Placebos are inert substances usually given to volunteers along with experimental drugs. By measuring the difference in responses to both the powerless placebo and the drug, the drug's effect is tested.

In a group of volunteers who had just had their wisdom teeth extracted, some of the subjects received morphine to alleviate their pain. The others received a placebo, which they believed to be morphine. Many of the placebo recipients said they experienced dramatic relief from their pain. However, when a drug that blocks the effects of the endorphin was given to them, the pain returned almost immediately. The test confirmed something that is very important to understand. When a placebo is given, and the individual believes he or she is getting relief, the brain releases chemicals to substantiate the belief. In many respects, the placebo effect is an act of faith.

If our thoughts can cause the brain to release adrenaline from the adrenal glands to help a 56-year-old heart patient lift an 1,800-pound pipe off a boy's head; and if our thoughts can produce natural endorphins that are fifty to one hundred ninety times as powerful as morphine, is it not possible for us to use this power of faith in our everyday lives, with the only side effect being happiness?

When people ask me why I'm so optimistic and high on life, I tell them, "I'm on endorphins."

They say, "It figures. We knew you were on something!"

The Incurable Optimist

Optimism is an incurable condition in the person with faith. Optimists believe that most disease, distress, disfunction, and disturbance can be cured. Optimists also are prevention oriented. Their thoughts and activities are focused on wellness, health, and success.

If you didn't have the opportunity to read *The Anatomy of an Illness: As Perceived by the Patient,* while it was a best-seller a couple of years ago, I highly recommend that you do. It was written by former *Saturday Review* editor, Norman Cousins, who was hospitalized in 1964 with an extremely rare, crippling disease. When conventional medicine failed to improve his condition and he was diagnosed as incurable, Cousins checked out of the hospital. Being aware of the harmful effects that negative emotions can have on the human body, Cousins reasoned that the reverse also must be true. He decided to dwell on becoming well again.

He borrowed a movie projector and prescribed his own treatment plan, consisting of Marx Brothers motion pictures and old "Candid Camera" reruns on film. He studied all aspects of his disease and with the help of his physician, learned what would have to take place in his body to make it "right" again. In his book he recounts that he "made the joyous discovery that ten minutes of genuine belly laughter would give me at least two hours of pain-free sleep." What had seemed to be a progressively debilitating, fatal cellular disease was reversed and, in time, Cousins almost completely recovered. After his personal account of his victory appeared in the *New England Journal of Medicine*, he received more than three thousand letters from appreciative physicians throughout the world. Thirty-four medical schools have included his article in their instructional materials and in 1978, Normal Cousins joined the faculty of the UCLA medical school.

Why Lee Trevino Is Always Lucky

Among my personal heroes is Lee Trevino, one of the all-time money winners on the PGA tour. In all of my lectures, in all of my seminars, and in all of my previous books, I have never failed to mention something that Lee Trevino has said or done that has inspired me or made me feel better.

On that fateful day when he and two other professional golfers were hit by lightning, he was heard to say after getting up from the ground: "Wow, I promise, Lord, I'll get my act together!" When a physician told him he shouldn't try to play in the U.S. Open, because his flu might get worse, his reply was: "Might get better . . . might even win!" (He came in second.)

As a boy, Trevino had been a caddy in San Antonio, Texas; he speaks fondly of his financial position then:

"We were so poor when I was a boy . . . if my mother threw the dog a bone, and the bone had any meat on it, the dog would call for a 'fair catch.' " He went on to say: "I used to be a poor Mexican, but now they think I'm a rich Spaniard."

I had the opportunity to play in the same foursome with him in the pro-am at one of the Andy Williams San Diego Open golf tournaments, which I was instrumental in developing to benefit the Salk Institute for Biological Studies. Trevino was so confident about his chipping and putting ability, that he used to make bets with his caddy as to how close to the pin he would chip, or whether he would sink a long putt. As he and his caddy approached the green, he would bargain: "I'll give you a thousand dollars if I don't chip out of the trap to within three feet of the pin; and, if I do, you will have given my golf bag a free ride." His caddy answered incredulously, "Do you think I'm crazy? What kind of odds are those?"

When asked how he thought he'd do in the Canadian Open, he quipped: "Are you kidding, that's my tournament!" That year, an inebriated spectator who was desperate to get Trevino's autograph jumped into the water hazard on the final hole, and started swimming across the pond toward the green. It was obvious to everyone that he was in no condition to make it. Lee Trevino stopped studying the break of the green for his putt, calmly strolled down to the water, pulled the drunk out, gave him a soggy autograph, ran back up to the green and sank his putt to win his third Canadian Open in four years!

Some people think Trevino is lucky. You and I know better. Luck lies at the intersection of preparation and opportunity. Since opportunity is always available, the individuals who are especially prepared always seem to win or reach their goals. The people who are unprepared rationalize their failure as "a run of bad luck," while labeling the winners as "lucky." Lee Trevino is one of those "lucky" individuals who is among the best prepared golfers ever to play the game, with a strong faith beyond himself. He's the most incurable optimist I have ever met.

Larry's Temporary Inconvenience

Another incurable optimist is Larry Robb. In the late 1960s he was one of the most successful stockbrokers in Texas. I met him in La Jolla and we hit it off right away. He was about as positive a thinker and doer as you could ever imagine. Larry was good looking, with a great sense of humor, incisive mind, earning well over a hundred thousand dollars a year; and to top it off he had a lovely wife and family. What more could a guy ask for?

Larry and I were flying from Dallas to San Diego one winter day and were discussing his uncanny ability to make money in a crazy stock market. When I asked him his secret, he sounded more like Will Rogers than a modern-day whiz kid. "I buy them low and sell them just before they peak or as they peak," he offered.

"What happens if they don't go up or if they peak and fall off the cliff?"

"I stay out of those deals," he winked.

I told him I would like to make some of that big, quick money, the way he did. He told me that if I would give him one thousand dollars to invest, he would give me three thousand dollars in six months. He got a little bolder and told me to invest four thousand dollars with him which he would convert into ten thousand dollars in twelve months. I sheepishly asked him what he could do with four hundred dollars. We laughed and agreed that it wouldn't even pay for my family to go skiing for one week at Lake Tahoe. We both loved to ski and fish and I envied the fact that he was on his way to Montana the following week for a long-awaited trip.

I didn't hear about the plane crash until a week after it had happened. The private aircraft had burned fiercely after impact and Larry had suffered third-degree burns over most of his body. He told me later that he had a choice to make as he was lying in the deep snow. Should he lie there peacefully and let nature take its course or should he try to get up and somehow find help? His surgeon told me later that the severity of his burns gave him a one-in-a-thousand chance of living.

Faith never ceases to amaze me. Larry remembered the name of Dr. Charles H. Williams, Chief of Anesthesiology at St. Joseph's Hospital in Houston, and called him. Dr. Williams notified Dr. Thomas Biggs, a friend of Larry's and a leading reconstructive surgeon, also in Houston. Dr. Biggs stayed on the telephone during the next several hours, giving instructions as to how to mix and administer the exact proportions of critical body fluids that would keep Larry alive. Dr. Williams flew to Montana in a chartered Lear jet and returned Larry to Houston, racing against the clock. It was touch and go for several weeks.

My first personal contact with Larry was by telephone. I'll never, in my life, forget what he said to me when he answered the phone at his bedside.

"Is that you, Denis?" I heard a familiar tone with a different enunciation.

"How are you doing, Larry?" I asked haltingly.

"I'm doing great, pal," the voice in my receiver said; "I've had a little, temporary inconvenience here that has slowed me down for a while . . . but no problem!"

I swallowed the waver in my voice and told him he was in my prayers and that I'd check back with him soon.

A few months had passed before I called again. I felt guilty for having sent cards instead of personally contacting him. Here was a good friend, lying near death, and I was too busy to try to bring some encouragement into his sterile world. His conversation nearly knocked me off my chair.

"I can talk a little more clearly now," he said; "the

scar tissue that was forming around my mouth has been removed surgically. I'm finally back at work. I've set up my office here in the hospital with an incoming and outgoing phone line, so I can sell on one line and still get incoming calls on the other."

All I could do was ask him how business was going. He told me it was a little slow, because now he was selling on sheer ability; whereas during his initial calls most of his business had come as the result of pity.

"I knew the pity wouldn't last more than a couple of weeks," he chuckled; "I've learned to chart the trends, since I can't sell stocks anymore by my good looks alone." As uncomfortable as it felt, I found myself laughing with Larry.

"It's Still Me Inside"

By the time I saw Larry in person, he had endured more than sixty operations. Even after a year, it was very difficult to look my buddy square in the face. He had been burned much more severely than I had anticipated. But to hear him talk about it, you would have thought he'd burned his fingers barbecuing in the backyard! I went to the therapist with him and watched him go through the excruciating pain of having his fingers pulled, bent, and massaged so he could move them properly and get the tendons stretching back in the right direction.

When he saw me hesitate to talk eye-to-eye, he said, "Don't worry, it's still me inside . . . just a temporary construction job going on at the surface." He told me that if you had faith and really knew yourself from the "inside-out," you wouldn't get discouraged when something unexpected came along to threaten you from the "outside-in." He said it was difficult for the people in his hometown to deal with his condition. To make it easier for the public, while he was going through the painful skin grafts and plastic reconstruction he wore a ski mask over his face in restaurants, banks, and stores. "They still laughed and stared at me," he reflected, "but it was more curiosity than revulsion as it had been before. Besides," he went on, "the ski mask got me motivated to get myself back in shape to hit the ski slopes!" I wondered how the bank tellers reacted the first time they saw him walk in with his ski mask on.

Here was a young man, with everything going for him, when suddenly his world literally went up in smoke. Why was he not crushed and broken? I thought about the thousands of young people who take their lives every year because they are depressed about their inability to cope with change. I thought about the thousands of complaints I have heard in my life from people who are just plain miserable. I thought that since misery loves company, the reason many people gripe so much about the conditions in their world is because they, subconsciously, want to bring the rest of us down to their own miserable level.

Larry proudly showed me the way the doctors had rebuilt his legs. They had grafted layers of skin tissue from other parts of his body to his calves and thighs. Although he was still walking with the aid of a cane when I first saw him, he soon discarded it as he built his leg strength back after hours and hours of bicycle riding. Today, Larry Robb is back to normal. Incredibly, he has total use of his hands and legs—he even skis—and is one of the most successful stockbrokers in Texas.

Flying back to San Diego, I stared out my window and tried to comprehend his unbelievable attitude. He figured that if you were born in despair, it would be tough to maintain your faith. But his belief was that since he had been born healthy, in America, with a strong spiritual faith, he wasn't going to let an accident discourage him. "It's much easier to get back to being who you know you are," he had said just before I had departed, "than it is to become like someone you don't know."

The following year I got a chance to apply what Larry taught me about faith. Our house on the hill in La Jolla burned down and we lost all of our material possessions. The important thing was that no lives were lost. Even the goldfish and the two turtles, Lightning and Streak, survived.

As the condolences poured in, I began to picture the new structure with a modern kitchen, walk-in closets, and a playroom for the kids. To this day whenever misfortune strikes, I can't seem to find much else to say other than, "No problem, we've had a little, temporary inconvenience."

Thank you, Larry.

Ten Action Steps to Optimism

1. Fly with the eagles. Don't run around with the Henny Pennys who are looking up, chanting, "The Sky is Falling!" Optimism and realism go together. They are the problem-solving twins. Pessimism and cynicism are the two worst companions. Your best friends should be individuals who are the "No problem, it's just a little, temporary inconvenience" type. As you help other people in need on a daily basis, also develop an inner circle of close associations in which the mutual attraction is not sharing problems or needs. The mutual attraction should be values and goals.

2. If you become depressed, visit any one of these four places: a children's hospital, a senior citizens' retirement home, the burn ward at a hospital, or an orphanage. If seeing people worse off than yourself depresses you more, take the positive approach. Take a walk by a playground or park where children are playing and laughing. Catch their spirit of wonder and adventure. Direct your thoughts toward helping others and renewing your faith. Visit your church or synagogue. Sometimes

even a change of location can change your thoughts and your feelings.

3. Listen to upbeat, inspiring music. When you are getting ready for work or school turn on the radio to a good FM station. Stay away from the morning TV news. You can brief yourself by scanning the news section on the front page of *The Wall Street Journal*. It will inform you of all you need to know about the international and national situation affecting your life. Read local news for interest concerning your profession and your family. Resist the temptation to waste time reading the sordid details of someone else's tragedies. Listen to music or cassette tapes in your car. If possible, have breakfast and lunch with an optimist. Instead of sitting in front of the TV at night, spend time listening to and being involved with those you love.

4. Change your vocabulary. Instead of, "I'm worn out," make it, "I'm relaxed, after an active day." Instead of, "Why don't they do something about it?" make it, "I know what I'm going to do." Instead of group griping, try praising someone in the group. Instead of, "Why me, Lord?" make it, "Try me, Lord." Instead of, "The world's a mess," make it, "I'm getting my own house in order."

5. "Remember the lobster." At a certain point in a lobster's growth, he discards his outer, protective shell and is vulnerable to all of his enemies. This continues until he grows a new "house" in which to live. Change is normal in life. With every change there is the unfamiliar and the unexpected. Instead of going into a shell, become vulnerable. Risk it! Reach inside for faith in things that are unseen.

6. Get high on yourself. Instead of, "Relief is just a swallow away," think of, "Belief will help you fol-

low the way." The people you associate with, the places you go, the things you listen to and watch, all are recorded in your thoughts. Since the mind tells the body how to act, think the highest and most uplifting thoughts you can imagine. When people ask you why you're so optimistic, tell them you're high. You are on endorphins!

7. Engage in positive recreation and education. Subscribe to cable TV programs specializing in the wonders of nature, family health, and cultural enrichment. Select the movies and television you watch for their quality and story value rather than their commercial appeal.

8. Visualize, think, and speak well of your health. Use positive self-talk on a daily basis. Don't dwell on your own small ailments such as colds, headaches, cuts, bruises, muscle pulls, sprains, and minor abrasions. If you pay too much attention to these occurrences they will reward you by becoming your best friends, coming often to pay their respects. What the mind harbors, the body manifests. This is especially important when you are raising children. Focus on the well family, and dwell on health as the usual environment around your house. I have seen more psychosomatic illnesses in homes where the parents dote on and smother the children with undue concern for their health and safety than in any other type of household. I believe in safety precautions and sound medical practice. I also believe that "your worst" or "your best" concerns will likely come to pass.

9. Call, visit, or write someone in need, every day of your life. Demonstrate your faith by passing it on to someone else.

10. Make Sunday "Good Faith" day. Get into the habit of attending church, listening, and sharing. According to the most recent studies on drug

abuse among teenagers and young adults, there are three cornerstones in the lives of those young individuals who do not use drugs of any kind: religious belief, family and extended-family relationships, and high self-esteem.

Questions about Your Faith

1. Do you expect success? What do you say to yourself?

2. Do you consider yourself healthy or "not so good"? What are you doing to stay fit?

3. Are you lucky? Why, or why not? Evaluate some recent experiences. How "lucky" were you? How prepared were you?

4. Do you tell people your problems? Why?

5. Do you get "high" or "low" on your thoughts? Think of some recent examples.

6. Would others view you as an optimist? Which of these statements would you use: The glass is half-full, or half-empty? It's a partly cloudy day, a partly sunny day?

8 | The Seed of Adaptability

TURNING PROBLEMS INTO OPPORTUNITIES

- **The Eighth Best-Kept Secret of Total Success**
- **Stumbling Blocks into Stepping-Stones**
- **Necessity—Mother of the Ice-Cream Cone**
- **The Birth of the Hot Dog**
- **The Opportunities of Mount St. Helens**
- **Motivation: The Two Faces of Stress**
- **How to Adapt and Live Longer**
- **Selye's Rules for Handling Stress**
- **Humor Yourself into Health and Happiness**
- **Ten Action Steps toward Adaptability**

These are troubled times. Many people bide their time and hope that the future will favor them with a brighter outlook. Others would gladly turn back the hands of time to "the good old days" when a haircut cost two bits, when the air was clean, and when life was uncomplicated and enjoyable.

Today if you pick up the newspaper and turn to the editorial page, you might read something like this:

> The world is too big for us. Too much going on, too many crimes, too much violence and excitement. Try as you will you get behind in the race, in spite of yourself. It's an incessant strain, to keep pace . . . and still, you lose ground. Science empties its discoveries on you so fast that you stagger beneath them in hopeless bewilderment. The political world is news seen so rapidly you're out of breath trying to keep pace with who's in and who's out. Everything is high pressure. Human nature can't endure much more!

This newspaper editorial reads like it could have been written last week, or last night. But it actually appeared more than one hundred fifty years ago, on June 16, 1833, in *The Atlantic Journal*. That was back in "the good old days."

What does it mean to you and me? What can we learn from this? I believe that this simple, tattered editorial, a century and a half old, teaches us one of the secrets of success.

The Eighth Best-Kept Secret of Total Success

When I speak to students at high school assemblies and commencement ceremonies throughout America, I love to tell them how it really is out there. The young generation destined to be our leaders of tomorrow cannot believe me when I tell them we are not going to "melt down" or "blow up." I tell them that they are the most fortunate pioneers in our history and that the changes they will witness will be more in one of their years, than in all of our grandparents' lives. Their eyes get as big as saucers when I tell them about the "good old days," which weren't really all that good.

The good old days I talk about to America's teenagers are the days of World Wars I and II, and the
Korean War. I talk about the turn of the century when
the horses were dying of cholera in the streets of New
York. I tell them about the great old days when we
used to take baths in a huge pan, using water that was
heated over a wood- or coal-burning stove. In those
good old days we bathed in the same water as those
who went before us. If you followed your uncle and, as
fate would have it, he was a pig farmer, instead of
getting ring around the collar, you got ring around the
person!

I tell our teenagers and young adults about the good
old days with polio, diphtheria, and scarlet fever. They
had never even heard of Jonas Salk! When I tell them
that we could not go to a community swimming pool or
a movie theater in the heat of the summer during the
1940s or early '50s for fear of becoming paralyzed or
crippled, or of dying from bulbar polio, they cannot
even begin to comprehend what I am relating. They
have never heard of the A, B, or C sticker you put on
your car windshield to buy a few gallons of gas per
month during gas rationing.

The kids look puzzled when I show them the headlines in the *Boston Globe* for November 13, 1857. The
headlines read: **"ENERGY CRISIS LOOMS."** Sub-
head: **"World to Go Dark? Whale Blubber Scarce!"** I
paint the scenario for the kids of the typical American
getting the morning paper on that grey, icy November
day, and getting hit by the headlines. "Hey, Martha,"
the guy might have yelled to his wife, "did you see the
morning paper? We've got the worst energy crisis in
recorded history!"

The kids begin to understand that there is too much
emphasis on what's wrong with our world. The way
their parents, teachers, and friends are complaining it
seems as if things are going from bad to worse. They
ask me about nuclear devastation and nuclear power
plants. My reply is honest. The Japanese are relying

heavily on nuclear energy and the Soviet Union generates nearly 60 percent of its power from nuclear energy plants. I am looking forward to laser fusion myself, rather than nuclear fission, which has more inherent dangers. I also believe what newscaster Paul Harvey says about our perspective on energy: "Had the first product using electricity been the electric chair, we would all be afraid to plug in our toasters!" As we look back into history we can always find the worst of times and the best of times. It all depends on what we are looking for.

The Eighth Best-Kept Secret of Total Success is that the good old days are here and now!

The main reason that "the good old days are here and now" is such a secret is that most people dwell on their current problems and remember the good times they had in the past. Another major reason it's such a well-kept secret is that most people don't learn from history that problems are normal. The most important reason, however, is that most people play up how awful conditions are today in order to justify their own lack of productivity and achievement.

Every generation laments its position as the one that is living under the most pressing and difficult circumstances in history. By complaining about the cruel world and sticking their heads in the sand, they never really have to roll up their sleeves and solve their problems. They can blame their problems on their elders or the government and pursue the new American diversion—"Escape Goat!" Escape Goat is a game in which everyone runs and hides and tries to find someone else willing to be "It."

In all of my lectures and seminars for youth, I tell our leaders of tomorrow that the good old days are now because these are the days of our lives. This is the only time in history in which we will be living. This is our time. I do not talk to them of rose-colored glasses or of gloom-colored glasses. I do not give them an overdose of Pollyanna. I speak to them of the inevitability of change.

Our eleven- and twelve-year-old athletes are breaking Olympic records set during my father's generation. Every day at the Mission Viejo Swim Club in Southern California our young swimmers break the gold medal winning performance set by Buster Crabbe (the screen's first Tarzan) at the Olympiad in Los Angeles in 1932. Our young men and women are getting taller, stronger, healthier, and smarter. Within five years, either the rules or the game of basketball will have to be changed to make the game more challenging again. It is beginning to get monotonous watching ten giants pounding up and down the courts "slam-dunking" the ball through the baskets at will.

The young people in my audience always ask me what we are going to do for energy when the petroleum is all gone. I tell them that my own generation has become more of a slave to technology than its master. I admit to them that in just a few decades we have used up half the world's fossil-fuel supplies, which took millions of years to be created. My generation has ignored the past and discounted the future, but we are finally aware of this. We tend to wait until we are facing a crisis before we take action. Instead of long-range planners, we have been acting like firemen!

Now that the Energy Crisis is acute and we have on our firemen's hats, we are beginning to seek solutions. In the foreseeable future, the use of laser fusion in just one power plant can take an energy source the size of a penny, combine it with sea water, and provide enough energy to power the western United States for three hundred fifty years. In the year 2020, our teenagers' children may have this kind of conversation with their parents: "You mean you used to drive those fossil-fuel automobiles back in the '80s and '90s?" the kids will ask their dad.

"Of course, we did," he will reply. "Things were tough back in those days. We used to have to drive to school!"

"You mean you *went* to school?" the teenagers gasp in disbelief.

"Yes, we did, back then," the father reminisces. "Your great-grandparents walked to school; we drove to school; and now you sit in front of the Apple 30 with the AT&T Videotext and take it all off the orbiting library's main line. We used to play an antique version of what you kids do for studies now, only we did it for fun in arcades. We called it Pac-Man and Frogger back then!"

In the year 2020, automobiles probably will be powered by an advanced battery pack for the short runs to and from offices and shopping. For the longer trips, cars will be powered by liquid-hydrogen engines. The exhaust from our future highway vehicles will be pure oxygen and steam, which are the by-products from burning liquid hydrogen. In effect, there will be tens of millions of rolling vacuum cleaners sucking the smog out of the cities and replacing it with air cleaner than the air above the Colorado Rockies. A big semitrailer will roar down the freeway, belching clouds of pure oxygen out of its stacks. There will be a sticker on the back of the truck with a new slogan: "Teamsters for Clean Air!"

I finish my lectures to the high school students by letting them in on the location for their grandchildren's senior prom. In the twenty-first century it will be common for proms to be held in foreign countries like Australia, which will be a popular choice. Australia will be a half-orbital shuttle run in twenty-nine minutes with a shuttle-busload of formally attired space travelers enjoying the spectacular, but brief panoramic view. They will go to Australia for the prom, but probably sneak over to Hong Kong for the after-prom, telling us they were in Australia with the chaperones the whole evening. Some things never change through the generations!

Stumbling Blocks into Stepping-Stones

We need to learn from that ancient Chinese definition of crisis that I use in all of my seminars. The Chinese symbols for *crisis* are identical to those for the word *opportunity*. Literally translated it reads, "Crisis is an opportunity riding the dangerous wind." The best way to adapt to change and lead a successful life is to view crises as opportunities, and stumbling blocks in your path as stepping-stones to the stars.

To develop adaptability to the stresses of life, you need to view those stresses as normal. Successful individuals develop mental toughness, commonly called strength of character. Research has proven that adversities and failures in our lives, if adapted to and viewed as normal corrective feedback, can help get us back on target. They serve to develop in us an immunity against anxiety, depression, and the adverse responses to stress.

The antianxiety drugs used increasingly in the United States today (over seventy million tablets consumed annually) lessen the emotional reactions to the threat of pain or failure; that is why we take them. But, unfortunately, they also interfere with the ability to learn to tolerate stress. It is far better to develop behavioral methods of coping with one's problems than to try to dissolve them with a pill.

History is full of interesting examples of individuals who have made their contributions to society while turning stumbling blocks into stepping-stones. O. J. Simpson wore leg braces as a boy in the streets of San Francisco. Beethoven was deaf. Milton was blind. Tom Dempsey kicked the longest field goal in NFL history with half a foot! There are thousands more who have transformed adversity into greatness.

Necessity—Mother of the Ice-Cream Cone

The Louisiana Purchase Exposition was held in St. Louis in 1904 in conjunction with the Olympic Games. Forty-two states and fifty-three nations took part in the exposition which celebrated the 100th anniversary of the transfer of the northern part of Louisiana from France to the United States. The exposition was popularly referred to as the St. Louis World's Fair.

Among the vendors at the Fair was a man with an ice cream concession and another with a hot waffle booth. As the crowds surged through the exhibits both the ice cream and waffle business flourished. On one particularly active day, the waffle vendor ran out of cardboard plates upon which he had been serving his waffles, with three different kinds of topping. He was dismayed to discover that no one in the exposition would sell him plates to replenish his supply. All the other vendors jealously hoarded their inventories, fearing that they might lose money as well.

The ice cream vendor expressed delight over his fellow concessionaire's plight. "That's the way the old waffle crumbles," he remarked. "It looks like you would be better off working for me selling ice cream."

The waffle vendor considered the alternative, which was attempting to serve his waffles without plates and watching the syrup run down the sleeves of his irate customers. He agreed to buy ice cream from the ice cream vendor at a discount and resell it at his booth, which was located down the arcade.

The waffle vendor tried to recoup his losses in the small profit margin he was making selling ice cream. His major problem was what to do with all the waffle batter ingredients in which he had invested his life savings to try to capitalize on the huge attendance at the St. Louis Fair. Suddenly an idea struck him like a bolt of lightning out of the blue. Why hadn't he thought of it before? He was certain it could work.

At home the next day, with the help of his wife, the

waffle vendor made a batch of one thousand waffles and pressed them thin with a flat iron. While they were still hot, he then rolled them into a circular pattern with a point at the bottom. The next morning he sold all of his ice cream before noon and all one thousand waffles, with three different toppings, as well! As a result of the stumbling block of running out of plates, he had been forced into inventing the "ice-cream cone."

The Birth of the Hot Dog

In the 1930s a German immigrant in Philadelphia was trying to make a living selling knockwurst and sauerkraut in his small restaurant. Being unable to afford plates and silverware like other establishments, he developed inexpensive cotton gloves for his patrons to hold the knockwurst, draped in sauerkraut, while they ate it. His major stumbling block came as the result of his customers' taking the gloves home with them for gardening and odd jobs around their homes. He nearly went broke trying to maintain a supply of gloves.

To solve the problem, he split a German roll down the center and placed the knockwurst and sauerkraut in the opening. As he served his clientele the first day, he explained that the split bun was taking the place of his serving gloves, which were being discontinued. One of the customers, spying the owner's dachshund snoozing in a corner of the restaurant, quipped, "Now we know why you're trying to cover up your knockwurst in that fancy roll. What happened to that other dog you used to have around here?" he laughed. In that instant the "hot dog" was born! And for years I thought it was invented by the owner of a baseball stadium to go with the great American pastime!

The Opportunities of Mount St. Helens

In 1980 the Pacific Northwest shuddered under the

devastating force of Mount St. Helens. The Cascade range was alive and restless again. It had been dormant for a number of years, but the silence was broken again and again as she continued to erupt and bring havoc to the surrounding communities. Television and newspaper reports from the area dominated the national news: "Forests annihilated, rivers choked, fish and wildlife destroyed, tourist areas buried, air poisoned, acid rain cloud moving eastward in the ionosphere, San Andreas Fault may be next, weather cycles may be permanently changed, only the beginning. . . ."

The purveyors of doom were making a fortune off Mount St. Helens. One million small plastic bags of "Mount St. Helens volcanic ash" were sold for a dollar a bag during the first week of the eruption. Everyone wanted to pass on a piece of the disaster to friends and relatives in other cities, or own it for posterity. The interesting thing about most of the bags of ashes is that the ashes came out of the promoters' fireplaces! A printer in Texas grossed nearly a million dollars on his four-color souvenir program of the first spectacular blast. During the next several weeks, throughout the United States, it seemed that everyone believed that the state of Washington was in deep ecological and economic trouble from which it might never recover.

Shortly after the biggest blast, I visited the area of Mount St. Helens; and less than a year later I revisited there. The impression I received was quite different from all the gloom and doom. The damage was overwhelming. No one would deny that. But what no one seems to have heard about are all the stepping-stones that have come from the stumbling blocks. Most of the salmon and steelhead managed to survive. Finding the rivers clogged with hot mud, volcanic ash, and debris. the fish followed alternate routes home, some of them less than six inches deep. Contrary to all expectations. scores of salmon selected unfamiliar estuaries to deposit their eggs at the end of their migration inland

They adapted their inherited instincts in order to survive.

The wildlife around Mount St. Helens returned quickly. Lakes and rivers soon were teeming with life, their waters full of rich, life-supporting nutrients generously supplied by the exploding volcano. Wild flowers bloomed as did tourist business in the area. Farmers who were wiped out by the thick layer of ash at least can be heartened by the fact that they have the richest mineral deposits in their soil on layaway for future crops. A geothermal plant has been planned in the area to utilize the molten rock to heat water, pumped beneath the surface, into superheated steam to drive turbines. Even Mount St. Helens is doing her part to help solve the Energy Crisis.

One of the most heartening reports regarding successful people's resiliency and adaptability to adversity came from the shareholders' meeting of one of our nation's largest lumber companies, located in the Pacific Northwest. The president of the company, addressing a somber group of investors at the annual meeting, said: "Ladies and gentlemen, I am happy to report that Mount St. Helens blew our trees down, stripped the bark, and sent them down to the mill with no labor in between. One more blast and we'll have a record year in earnings!" Obviously, the company had to double-plant new forests-that would take years to grow to the size of those that had been destroyed. The capital investment required to offset the volcano's impact would be tremendous. The point, however, is how to convert Mount St. Helens into "opportunity riding the dangerous wind" and to turn lava piles from stumbling blocks into stepping-stones to success.

A short poem on my office wall reminds me of the importance of adaptability in life. It was written by Gail Brook Burket and is one of my favorites:

> I do not ask to walk smooth paths
> Nor bear an easy load,

I pray for strength and fortitude
To climb the rock-strewn road.

Give me such courage I can scale
The hardest peaks alone,
And transform every stumbling block
Into a stepping-stone.[1]

Motivation: The Two Faces of Stress

When Peter Benchley was filming the movie *Jaws*,
based upon his best-selling novel, he went to Australia
to observe sharks firsthand, in their natural environment. While observing and filming them, he was standing chest-deep in the ocean just offshore. When he
noticed one coming alarmingly close to him and apparently in his direction, he turned and ran in the water
toward the beach. Have you ever tried running chest-
deep in water? Benchley said trying to run in that position was like "dancing on peanut butter."

I have thought about that statement many times
since I first heard about the incident. I think that is
what most people are doing with their lives. They are
very busy, but they don't seem to be getting anywhere. They are just going through the motions as if
they were "dancing on peanut butter." Most people
settle for the path of least resistance and the safest way
rather than take the calculated risk. Since the media
are always bombarding our senses with "bad news,"
most individuals find solace in watching and hearing
about the problems of others as justification for their
own lack of effort.

Not long ago a television station conducted an experiment. It concentrated on "good news" reporting.
The experiment only lasted six weeks due to lack of
audience viewing and commercial sponsorship. Can

---

1. Burket, Gail Brook, *Special Days to Remember* (St. Louis:
O'Neal Publishing, 1980), p. 125.

you imagine anything as distressful as coming home from another boring, frustrating day of work and plopping in front of the TV to watch inspirational, true, human interest stories of people achieving in these trying times? One report was about a family of Viet Nam boat people who had made a fortune with a chain of fast food Chungking restaurants since their arrival in the United States. How do you think that kind of story made most people feel after the evening TV anchorman has just told the audience that no one can make it in this economy?

I believe that "bad news" on television and the sensation soaps such as "Dallas," "Dynasty," "Flamingo Road," "Falcon Crest," and "General Hospital" are so appealing and popular to the general audience because they demonstrate human beings at their worst. With a steady diet of this kind of input, most people can easily rationalize their own life-style of "dancing on peanut butter." After all, they certainly are living more normal lives than those they see every night on television.

A four-hundred-pound gorilla named Willy B living in the Atlanta zoo is a TV addict. The zoo officials have installed several sets that he can watch during the day. Thousands of zoo visitors file by to watch Willy, watching TV. Researchers who have been studying Willy's viewing habits closely have come to the astounding conclusion that Willy's favorite shows match those that also are the favorites of the American general public. That tells us something about our taste in entertainment! However, that statement may be unfair to Willy the gorilla. He doesn't have anything else to do!

Everyone is motivated a little or a lot to do something or nothing. Motivation is the internalized drive toward the dominant thought of the moment. By definition, motivation is "motive in action."

The fear of change or risk causes most people to "dance on peanut butter" and forfeit their games of life. Two other more active kinds of motivation drive our lives and have much more significant mental and physical effects. These are "Penalty Motivation" and "Reward Motivation." I call them the two faces of stress.

"Penalty Motivation" tells you to do something or there will be a penalty to pay. These options are better known as compulsion (have to) and inhibition (can't) and there is always a penalty (or else).

"Reward Motivation" tells you to seek something because there will be a reward for success. It also tells you that you are able to do it. These options are better known as propulsion (want to) and volition (can) and there is always a reward (benefit).

Both "Penalty Motivation" and "Reward Motivation" cause stress. "Penalty Motivation," associated with feelings of compulsion and inhibition, causes negative stress known as "distress." Distress leads to disorientation, distortion, discomfort, disfunction, and disease. "Reward Motivation," associated with feelings of propulsion and volition, causes positive stress known as "eustress." Eustress leads to goal orientation, energy, power, and a sense of well-being.

Is stress good or bad then? The answer is yes, stress is either good or bad, depending on whether you are motivated by "penalty of failure" or motivated by "reward of success." Which is it for you?

How to Adapt and Live Longer

One of the most meaningful personal and professional relationships I have had in my life was my friendship with the late Dr. Hans Selye. Dr. Selye, who died in 1982, is the acknowledged "father of stress." As a young doctor who emigrated from Central Europe to Canada in the 1930s, he first borrowed the English word *stress* from physics to describe the body's responses to everything from viruses and cold temperatures, to emotions such as fear and anger. Dr. Selye's definition of stress, nearly fifty years old, is still the best explanation of what it really is: "Stress is the body's nonspecific response to any demand placed on it, whether that demand is pleasant or not."

I first met Hans Selye in 1976 in Sarasota, Florida, shortly before his 70th birthday. In the seven years that I knew him, I always considered him as a little boy, with curious eyes, inside the body of an older man. As president of the International Society for Advanced Education, I arranged for Dr. Selye and Dr. Jonas Salk to be the keynote speakers at the International Stress Symposium in April of 1976 in Sarasota's beautiful Van Wezel theater. After that first lecture, I was so fascinated with his approach to stress that I made many trips to visit Selye at his research facilities at the Institute of Experimental Medicine and Surgery in Montreal. Over a period of five years, I audiotaped and videotaped our interviews, which I consider to be among my most priceless personal possessions. I have always been one to collect and share treasured moments, rather than material objects or things.

Hans Selye had a way of being able to explain complex scientific data by the use of easy-to-understand examples. Inasmuch as stress has become our national preoccupation and the newsstands are flooded with thousands of articles extolling some new formula for conquering it, I would like to share my recollections of the essence of what I learned from Hans Selye.

Dr. Selye usually discussed the two faces of stress. He observed that sitting in a dentist's chair or kissing passionately can be equally stressful—however, not equally agreeable. He said that when a mother suddenly hears that her son has died in battle, she will show all the biochemical changes characteristic of stress. Under stress, there is a need for bodily movement. In addition, the mucous lining of the stomach starts to dissolve, the body loses weight, the adrenal glands lose their store of hormones, and the individual suffers from insomnia. These are all nonspecific responses. However, the specific effect of that news is great pain and suffering.

A few years later this same son walks into her living room, perfectly healthy. The news had been false; nothing had happened to him. The mother will experience extreme joy. The specific effects of this experience are very pleasant. However, the nonspecific stress is just the same as in the case of the bad news! It is not the physical stimulus that makes the difference; it is the attitude with which we take it.

One evening when we were sitting in Dr. Selye's study, I told him my father had given me my first lesson in how to cope with stress at the age of twelve. My father managed a warehouse until his death in 1982. Although he was never highly salaried and had little formal education, he was one of the wisest men I knew. When I would go to bed at night, my dad would come and sit with me for a while and chat with me. These are the most important moments that a father and son can spend together; those precious minutes before going to sleep. He would always give me something inspirational to sleep on.

When he left my room, after tucking me in, he would "blow" out my light, as if by magic. I didn't see his hand flick off the switch from behind his back. All I remember is his marvelous power to blow it out like a candle on a cake.

After my room became dark he would always say: "Good night, my son. Always remember that when your light goes out, it goes out all over the world. Light and life are in the eyes of the beholder. Keep your eyes bright and open to the light in the darkness. Life is what *you* make it . . . it makes little difference what is happening . . . it is how *you* take it that counts!"

I told Hans Selye that those words my father had given me as a boy had stayed with me all of my adult life, like a beacon in the fog. Selye told me that my father's philosophy matched his own. He said that he had condensed twenty years of research into a 300-

page book, *The Stress of Life*. When McGraw-Hill told him his explanations were still too long and complicated, he boiled his research down to a ten-page summary. When the editor told him it was still too complex, he decided to make it short and simple enough for everyone to understand: "Fight for your highest attainable aim; but never put up resistance in vain."

Selye's Rules for Handling Stress

Dr. Selye gave me three basic rules for understanding his theories on the stress of life:[2]

1. *Find your own purpose in life, that fits your own personal stress level.* Most of us fit into two main categories. There are the "racehorses" who thrive on pressure and are only happy with life in the fast lane. Then, there are the "turtles" who in order to be happy require a more paced, tranquil environment—something that would bore or frustrate most racehorse types. If you force a racehorse not to move, give him all the leisure, all the food he wants, all the luxury, after a while he can't run any more. Unused organs atrophy. You need to work; it's built into your system. You need an outlet for your talents and for your energies. But, if you tried to teach a turtle to run as fast as a racehorse, you would kill it.

   Most of us are trying to be racehorses. We charge through our lives as if life were a race to finish first. The real mission is to find a purpose that we can respect. It needs to be *our* goal—not the goal of our parents, or our friends, but our own personal, indi-

---

2. The material on these pages is taken from the author's taped interviews with Dr. Selye at the Institute of Experimental Medicine, University of Montreal, Canada, August 29, 30, 1976.

vidual goal. One way to determine whether you are on the right track is to define your own meaning of "work." We all seem to clamor for shorter working hours and larger incomes. What is work and what is leisure?

If work is what you have to do, then leisure is what you want to do. A professional fisherman who has been out to sea and is exhausted coming home will do some gardening and relax in the evening. The professional gardener, conversely, probably will go out fishing to get away from his work. Although we all need diversion, you have to be certain that you enjoy your profession sufficiently to call it a "play" profession. Dr. Selye said he never did a stitch of work in his life, although he was up at five each morning and worked until late at night. He said he "played" all the time because to him research was play. This kind of attitude is possible for all of us to develop more.

2. *Control your emotional level by recognizing situations as being either life-threatening or non-life-threatening. Respond, rather than react.* There is a psychological myth that venting your anger is the healthy thing to do. The problem with venting anger is that you can't take back what you said or did to the person receiving it. The act of venting anger becomes habit forming. Ask any wife or mother who has been a victim of a husband's or a child's tantrums. Ask any child who has been abused by habitually irate parents. *Anger can result from threatened values.* Most people who display a lot of anger have low self-esteem. They look at every divergent opinion as a put-down and a personal threat.

Within the body are two types of chemical messengers: the so-called messengers of peace (the doves), which tell the tissues not to fight because it's not worth it; and the messengers of war (the hawks) which tell the body to destroy invading foreign substances and fight.

The messengers of peace are called "syntoxic" hormones (from the Greek *syn*—together; as in *symbiosis,* living together, and *synergy,* working together). These hormones tell the tissues to take it easy, it isn't worth fighting. If you don't put up any fight, you won't be sick. They know that it is not this intruder, but the fight that will make you sick.

The messengers of war are called "catatoxic" hormones. Their mission is to search and destroy dangerous invaders that are life-threatening. They stimulate the production of various enzymes which destroy substances in the body. The problem with people who react to everyday life confrontations with this "fight or flight" catatoxic reaction is that they are spending their energies on the wrong causes.

All of us have a "stress" savings account deposited in our bodies as our life-force. The object is to spend it wisely over the longest time span possible. The difference between our "stress" savings account and a normal bank account is that we cannot make any more deposits into the "stress" account. We can only make withdrawals. The reason most people age at such different rates is that our society is full of "big spenders" who overreact to harmless circumstances as if they were life-or-death matters. We see it every day on our freeways on the way to work.

Real maturity is in knowing when to behave syntoxically and when to react catatoxically. If you go out in the evening and meet a drunk, he may shower you with insults. Recognizing that he is a harmless, but obnoxious, drunk you take a syntoxic attitude and pass him by, saying nothing. He's so drunk he can't attack his own bar stool. You adapt to the annoyance and no trouble results.

What if you were to misinterpret the situation as life-threatening and treat him, instead, as if he were a homicidal maniac? Without thinking, you react with a surge of bodily resources. Into your blood flash adrenal secretions that muster strength from sugar and stored fats, stimulating pulse, respiration, and blood pressure. Your digestive processes turn off at once and the protective lining of the stomach starts to dissolve, as all of the blood rushes to the battle zones. Your coagulation chemistry prepares to resist wounds with quick clotting. The alarm system is in red alert!

Even if you don't actually fight, you can drop dead on the spot if you are predisposed to coronary failure. In this case the stress of preparing for battle is what killed you. Consider that carefully. Who was the murderer? The drunk didn't touch you. You killed yourself. How many people are killing themselves or aging prematurely, because they are not aware of the consequences of their behavior?

By not being aware, you could also have misunderstood the situation in an opposite sense. You observe an individual displaying irrational behavior and you mistake him for a harmless drunk. Actually, he is a homicidal maniac with a dagger in his hand. In this case, the correct behavior would have been to sound the alarm and trigger your "fight or flight" stress mechanism. There is imminent physical danger and you either need to disarm him or flee the scene to survive. This is why it is important to evaluate your daily problems as to whether they are really dangerous or nondangerous.

Ninety percent of our confrontations in life are with imaginary predators. We "stew in our own juices" and do battle with ourselves because the appropriate response to most of our daily problems is neither to fight nor take flight. Since there is nowhere to run to and no one we can hit, most of us are caught in an "invisible entrapment" which can lead to a host of stress-related diseases.

It is better to learn to adapt to and live with situations than to react in a state of alarm and resistance. Alarm and resistance as a life-style lead to early exhaustion. Emotionally upset individuals literally withdraw all of their energy reserves ahead of schedule and run out of life too soon.

3. *Collect the goodwill and appreciation of others.* The absence of hate and the presence of love seem to inspire the right kind of energy, or "eustress." Eustress links the Greek prefix for *good* with stress *(eu-stress)* in a similar way to *euphoria* and *euphonia.* The more we modify our self-centeredness and built-in selfishness, the more other people will accept us. The more acceptance we have from others, the safer we feel and the less negative stress we have to endure.

Dr. Selye's observation was that one of the most effective keys to living is to persuade others to share our natural desire for our own well-being. He said this can be done only by making a constant effort to win the respect and gratitude of our fellowmen and women. Selye rephrased the biblical quote, "Love thy neighbor as thyself," into his own personal code of behavior: "Earn thy neighbor's love." Rather than trying to accumulate money or power, he suggested that we acquire goodwill by doing something that helps our neighbor. "Hoard goodwill," Dr. Selye advised, "and your house will be a storehouse of happiness."

The last time I saw Hans Selye was in a hotel room in Canada early in 1982. As usual, he was full of optimism and enthusiasm. He will always be a sundial in my life. One of his favorite poems is a folk proverb he often heard while growing up in Austria and Hungary. He told me it helped him to never carry grudges and to quickly forget unpleasant incidents:

> Imitate the sundial's ways,
> Count only the pleasant days.

Humor Yourself into Health and Happiness

In the previous chapter we talked about optimism and faith. We learned that Norman Cousins overcame an incurable disease by laughing and dwelling on getting well again. Regardless of the healing qualities, isn't it fun to laugh a lot? I love to laugh. I am not so much turned on by contrived comedy routines or a steady stream of one-liners. I enjoy the real, true humor of everyday life. Humor is laughing at yourself, when you have been taking yourself too seriously. Humor is laughing at life in general.

Oscar Wilde said: "People are never so trivial as when they take themselves very seriously." I like humor according to Andy Rooney, who can even find something humorous about the Internal Revenue Service.

There is something amazing about individuals who have lived eighty years or more. Many of them seem to have a great sense of humor. Norman Vincent Peale, Maurice Chevalier, Rose Kennedy, Lowell Thomas, Bob Hope, and George Burns are prime examples. Although Art Linkletter has nearly a decade to go before he reaches his prime at 80, he is one of the few people in the world who has remained in touch with children at their own level, throughout his adult life. Danny Kaye is perhaps the only other person I have seen who can relate to kids as well as Art Linkletter can.

About every two months I appear at Positive Living rallies throughout the country along with Art Linkletter, Paul Harvey, Zig Ziglar, Robert Schuller, and Norman Vincent Peale. Spiritual faith and humor are the two cornerstones that make each of these platform personalities among the greatest in our country. I always enjoy being on the same program with all of them. I especially enjoy my friendship with Art Linkletter and his brand of humor that keeps him ageless.

Art has found the secret to youth: He looks at life through the eyes of a child. When Art speaks to America, he encourages all of us to laugh at ourselves and to find the child within each of us. When children grow up, they get old. Art encourages us not to grow up. He reminds us of our youth by recounting some of the "serious" interviews he has had through the years with children on his shows. To me they are the essence of what honest humor is all about.

At the rallies, as the keynote speaker before ten thousand people, Art Linkletter reminds us that "kids say the darnedest things." He remembers a three-year-old girl with big, brown eyes whom he asked, "What do you do to help your mother?" "I help my mom cook brefas," she replied eagerly. "And what do you do to help your mom with breakfast?" Art asked. She didn't hesitate: "I put the toast in the toaster, but she won't let me flush it!"

When Art asked one grammar school youth what his father did for a living, the boy took to the microphone as if it were an ice-cream cone. "My Dad's a cop," the boy began. "He catches crooks, and burglars, and spread-eagles them, and puts the cuffs on them, and takes them down to the station, and puts them in jail!" "Wow," Art replied, "I'll bet your mother gets worried about his work, doesn't she?" "Heck no," the youth assured Art, "he brings her lots of watches and rings and jewelry. She doesn't mind his work at all!"

The story I like most is the one Art tells about the lad to whom he gave a hypothetical problem to solve on one of his shows. "Let's say," Art began, "that you are a commercial airline pilot, flying to Hawaii, with 250 passengers in the back, and your engines quit. What would you do in a situation like that, if you were the pilot?" The boy thought for a moment and then came out with his solution: "I'd put the fasten-seat-belt sign on and then parachute!" He seemed proud of his answer, until he heard the studio audience laughing. He put his hands in his pockets and tears began to well up in his eyes. Art came quickly and gently to his rescue. "That was a great answer, Son. They weren't laughing at *you,* they were happy with what you said," Art consoled. The boy still didn't look satisfied, as he replied: "Yes, but I was coming right back to the plane. I was just going to get some gas!"

Let's you and I adapt to the ups and downs in life by maintaining our sense of humor. Let's keep the child alive and awake within us. Remember, you know that you're growing older when your children look middle-aged . . . when you get winded playing video games . . . when your pacemaker makes the garage door open every time an attractive young person goes by . . . and when the little grey-haired person you help across the street is your own spouse!

You and I will never grow old as long as we can see the wonder of life through the eyes of a child. Little children seem to find as much fun in the cardboard cartons that package their toys as they do in the toys themselves. Children laugh at almost anything— puppies and other animals, bugs, butterflies, sprinklers, piñatas, merry-go-rounds, and their own faces in the mirror.

As long as we can look at ourselves through the eyes of a child and not take ourselves too seriously we have learned the essence of adaptability. Since change is inevitable we know that tomorrow will bring a new surprise, a new challenge, and a new delight. We look forward to the promise of each day, having discovered the secret that the good old days are here and now.

Ten Action Steps toward Adaptability

1. Examine your sense of humor to determine how it has served you. Is it mainly a warehouse for jokes and anecdotes, or does it function—as it should—to help you perceive your own occasionally ludicrous aspects?

2. Take responsibility for your emotions. When you begin to get angry, acknowledge the fact that you own your emotions. Remove yourself from a potentially hostile situation. When you talk about your anger or dissatisfaction, say, "I feel angry when I see that happening," instead of saying, "You make me angry when you do that." Only you can make you angry.

3. When you reprimand someone or express your unhappiness, try to do so after the urge to fight or become upset has subsided. The best way to get your feelings across is when you can speak in a normal voice, without all of the warlike body language. When you are upset, try a substitute physical exercise such as running, tennis, racquetball, or handball, in which there is impact involved to release the built-up adrenaline in your system. Do speak your mind, but criticize the behavior without attacking the other person.

4. There is no such thing as winning an argument. There is only winning an agreement.

5. View change as normal. Constantly monitor and evaluate your capacity for change of pace, for flexibility, for new ideas, for surprises, and for rapid adaptability to change.

6. Don't engage in "all or nothing" management. If things don't work out exactly the way you had planned them, salvage a good situation. Don't be like the number one team that loses one game and

thinks the entire season was a total failure. Don't look for unrealistic perfection in others or yourself. It will cause you to discredit your performance continually, and whatever you do will rarely measure up.

7. Let other people take responsibility for their own behavior. Don't engage in the game of self-blame or false guilt, when others close to you cause negative effects in their lives. Beyond reasonable respect for the law and personal safety, even your own children are in charge of their own lives. Build adaptability into your home and work situation, so that courage and flexibility are two solid factors.

8. Learn to say "no" as if it means "yes, I am already committed." One of the best ways to relieve stress is to schedule your time so that you can, comfortably, keep the commitments you make. Being "under the gun" all the time is characteristic of so-called Type A behavior, which increases the risk for coronary and other stress-related diseases. Saying "no" in advance is much less painful than admitting "I'm sorry I couldn't deliver" later on. Only you can place yourself under the gun.

9. Simplify your life. Get rid of the clutter and the nonproductive activities. Continue to ask yourself, at least once per week, "Beyond the normal routine of my daily work and schedule, what is the essence of my life and what do I really want to be spending my time on?"

10. Engage in inspirational recreation. Get out the kites, grab the Frisbees, dust off the picnic basket, share a project with the children, attend little theater productions, musicals, and concentrate most of your television- and movie-viewing on shows that warm your heart.

Questions about Your Adaptability

1. Do you wish times were like they used to be? What are telltale phrases you hear coming from yourself or others?

2. Can you adapt easily to change? Think of some examples of how you have faced change recently.

3. Do you feel pressured by life? What do you do to let off steam? Do you do it regularly, on a planned basis, or do you have to "blow up"?

4. Are you in a rut? If so, try to describe the rut. What makes your job, or other parts of your life-style, a "rut"?

5. Do little things bother you? What kind? When? Try to identify what the little things are, and what you can do about them.

6. Can you laugh at your mistakes? Ask your spouse or close friends if they think you do.

9 | The Seed of Perseverance

THE WILL TO WIN IS EVERYTHING

- **The Ninth Best-Kept Secret of Total Success**
- **Wilma Came from Behind**
- **You've Got to Start Somewhere**
- **Always Go for the Gold**
- **A Living Legend**
- **What Vince Lombardi Really Said**
- **The Secret behind Those Golden Arches**
- **It's Never Too Late to Try**
- **Ten Action Steps toward Perseverance**

We have already talked about the Seed of Faith in an earlier chapter. The Seed of Perseverance is similar, but it is different in that it is the *test* of Faith. Perseverance is hanging in there when the odds stack up against you, but you know you're right.

One of the most fundamental character traits common to all successful individuals whom I have studied, is that they all believe in God. Each of them believes he or she is an integral part of God's plan. With this belief in the order and ongoing promise of the universe, they have been able to develop creative imaginations, self-esteem, wisdom, goals, and a deep faith in their convictions and commitments. Their faith has been the strong root system that has allowed them to bend and grow with the winds of change without their spirits breaking. This ability to bend and spring back is demonstrated in their unusual adaptability and in their habit of looking at the bright side of even the darkest situation.

The Ninth Best-Kept Secret of Total Success

Maybe that's why real success is such a well-kept secret. Everyone wants it. Most people spend countless days and years dreaming about it. Everyone talks, writes, visualizes it, and goes to meetings to hear more about it. But very little happens to make it happen. Why? People say they are putting their faith in a miracle. But miracles have been proven to be *faith in action*. When someone says "What has happened is a miracle," he usually follows in the next breath with, "our prayers were answered," and "we never gave up hope that if we just kept on working, we would see it through."

> **The Ninth Best-Kept Secret of Total Success is that winners work at doing things the majority of the population are not willing to do.**

You'll notice that I said "work at" doing things that others are "not willing" to do. I did not say "not able" to do. I said "not willing." An individual who will not read or learn or work or pray is the real loser in the game of life. Those who cannot read or learn or work or even pray, because of a disability or oppressive environment, are not losers. They are heroes and heroines in the struggle just to get to the starting line. The losers in life are those who want to look like, earn like, dress like, take time off like, travel like, own like, retire like and be like somebody else. They are losers by default, rather than by defeat in the arena of life. In America there is no excuse for default and despair. We throw out in our garbage every week what the people of the underdeveloped countries eat in a year. One Thanksgiving dinner for an American family of five would feed twenty starving citizens of one of the underdeveloped nations for a month.

No socioeconomic condition in this country will disallow the planting and nurturing of Seeds of Greatness. As the powerful character actor in the recent Rocky movie, Mr. "T" of *Rocky III,* puts it straight out on the table, "I may have been raised in the ghetto, but there ain't no ghetto in me."

Yes, there is poverty, discrimination, ignorance, bigotry, injustice, and irony in this country. And, yes, there is opportunity, determination, information, openness, justice and faith in this country. What is needed is this "best-kept secret" called perseverance. Show me someone who has succeeded in the face of incredible odds, and I will show you a person who knows that perseverance makes the difference.

Wilma Came from Behind

Wilma was willing to work at doing things that the majority of the population are not willing to do. Her first vivid thought as a six-year-old was "I'm going to travel out of this small town and make my place in the world." It's true that she already had experienced some travel early in her life. The Nashville hospital, forty-five miles to the south, had become her home away from home.

Born prematurely, with complications that resulted in her contracting double pneumonia twice, and scarlet fever, Wilma did not get what you'd call a head start in life. A bout with polio had left her left leg crooked and her foot twisted inward. The leg braces always seemed like such a nuisance. All of this made it difficult to compete with her brothers and sisters in the race to the dinner table!

She recalls her bus rides to Nashville for the treatments, which continued for six more years. On the trip down to the hospital she would imagine herself living in the stately, white, colonial house on the hill. At the hospital she would always ask the doctor, sometimes three or four times during each visit, "When will I get to take these braces off and walk without them?" Careful not to raise false hopes, he always said, "We'll see."

On the bus trip home she would visualize herself being a parent, with happy children around her. She would tell her mother of her dreams to make a special contribution in life and to go out and experience the world. Her mother, loving and supportive, would listen patiently and reassure her in those indelible words, "Honey, the most important thing in life is for you to believe it and keep on trying."

She began to believe, by age 11, that she would take those braces off some day. The doctor wasn't so sure, but he did suggest that Wilma's legs should be exercised a little. Wilma decided that a lot of exercise would be much better than a little exercise. The family had strong Christian roots as Southern Baptists, and being honest was a virtue she had always practiced. However, just in this one matter, she admits, she "massaged the truth" a little.

As she continued her back-and-forth routine to the hospital, her mother and father sometimes would take a different child in the family along. The doctor was able to teach each of them how to give Wilma's legs daily exercise. But Wilma's idea of massage was different from the doctor's. When her parents would leave the house, one of her brothers or sisters would be stationed at the door as a "watcher." She would take the braces off every day and painfully walk around the house for hours. If anyone would come in, the lookout would help her back on the bed and go through the motions of massaging her legs, to justify the braces being off. This continued for about a year and, though her confidence was growing, so also was a gnawing feeling of guilt inside of her. She wondered how to tell her mother of this unauthorized, do-it-yourself rehabilitation program.

During her next routine visit to Nashville, Wilma decided "judgment day" had come. She told the doctor, "I have something I'd like to share with you." She proceeded to take the braces off and walked across the office to where he was sitting. She could feel her mother's eyes behind her as she walked, knowing that the actions that had brought her to this miraculous moment were strictly against house rules.

"How long have you been doing this?" the doctor questioned, trying to control his surprise.

"For the past year," she said, trying not to look directly at her mother. "I . . . sometimes . . . take the braces off and walk around the house."

"Well, since you've been honest in sharing this with me," the doctor replied, "sometimes I'll let you take them off and walk around the house." "Sometimes" was the only permission she needed. She never put them on again.

You've Got to Start Somewhere

As Wilma turned 12, she discovered that girls run and jump and play, just like boys. She had been pretty much housebound and people always had to come to visit her. As she began to explore her new, expanded horizon, she decided that she would conquer anything that had to do with girls' athletics. One of her sisters, Yvonne, who was two years older, was trying out for the girls' basketball team. She decided to try out, too, thinking it would be fun to be able to play on a team with her sister. She was crushed to learn that out of thirty girls trying out she wasn't even one of the twelve finalists. She ran home vowing that she would show them all that she was good enough. Oh, how she wanted to show the kids, who had never played with her, that she was good enough!

When she arrived home, she noticed the coach's car in the driveway. "Oh, no," she thought, "he won't even let me break the news to my own parents that I didn't make the team!" She ran around to the back door and entered the house quietly. She pressed against the kitchen door to hear the conversation in the living room.

The coach was busy explaining what time her sister would be home from practice, how many road trips they would take, who would chaperone, and all the details parents need to know when their daughter has made the team. Her father was not a man of many words, but, when he spoke, you knew it was the law. "There's only one stipulation for my approval of Yvonne joining your team," her father said. "Anything you want," assured the coach. "My girls always travel in twos," her father said slowly, "and if you want Yvonne, you'll have to take Wilma along as her chaperone." It wasn't exactly what she had in mind, but it was a start!

Wilma soon found out that being placed on a team by your father and being selected for the team by the coach were two entirely different things. She could feel the resentment of the twelve other girls; but she also was exhilarated when she saw the uniforms. They were beautiful, new, black and gold satin. There's something about your first uniform when you play Pop Warner, or Little League, or become a Girl Scout, or join the service; it creates a special feeling of identity. You belong, when you put on that uniform. They ran out of new uniforms by the time they got to her, so they gave her a green and gold one from the old batch. "Never mind," she thought, as she sat on the end of the bench throughout the season, "I'll get my chance."

She finally got the nerve to confront her coach with her magnificent obsession. The six-foot, eighty-nine-pound straggler came into his office and found him as he always seemed to be, a little gruff and very direct. "Well, what do you want?" he asked. She forgot her prepared speech and just stood there shifting her weight from one foot to the other. "Speak up," he said, "people who have important things to say, get them said! If you don't state what it is, I will never know what your problem is."

She finally blurted out, "If you will give me ten minutes of your time, and only ten minutes—every day—I will give you in return a world class athlete."

He laughed, uncontrollably, not certain he had heard correctly the audacity of her words. As she turned to leave, he stopped her. "Wait a minute," he said. "I'll give you the ten minutes you want, but remember I'm going to be busy with *real* world class athletes, people who are getting scholarships and going off to college."

She was so excited that she wore her gym clothes to school every day, underneath her street clothes. When the bell would ring, she was the first kid in the gym to receive her precious gift of ten minutes of personal instruction. It became obvious right away that most of the instruction was to be verbal and that she was making little progress translating the words into real basketball skills. As she sat crying, two boys whom she had known for a long time came up and tried to comfort her.

"I really can't understand why it's so hard for me to do what he tells me. I need help," she said softly.

"We'll go with you for the ten-minute session and then help you practice what the coach is trying to teach you," they volunteered.

The next day they began. Wilma's best girl friend joined in so that they could play two-on-two, half-court basketball. Day after day they would listen and practice, listen and practice—mastering the game of basketball.

When Wilma and her girl friend were selected for the team the following year, they both wondered if they could measure up to the real thing, compared to their playground practice. As the inseparable pair discussed their mutual dreams and fears, they decided that the only thing they could do was to *do their very best*. They agreed that if their very best was not good enough, or if they could not cope with the situation, they would be grateful for the experience and walk away from it, having gained something meaningful for the rest of their lives. Every morning during the season they would run excitedly to look in the newspaper, to see what had been reported about their performance the previous night. As was becoming routine news, Wilma's friend was number one and she was number two.

Always Go for the Gold

While she was running up and down the courts that year, trying to outduel her girl friend in their "Avis and Hertz" friendly competition for top billing, someone else was watching her. Her high school referee at every game was unknown to her, but he was Ed Temple, the internationally known track coach of the prestigious Tigerbelles of Tennessee State University (Nashville). Under his tutoring some of the Tigerbelles had developed into the fastest women in the country. Temple asked for volunteers from the basketball team who would be interested in trying out for a girl's track team. Wilma's reasoning was basic: "Basketball season is over, which means no more games or practices . . . which means more time for chores at home. Why not volunteer for the track team?"

The first time Wilma ran a race, she found she could beat her girl friend. Then she beat all the other girls in her high school—then, every high school girl in the state of Tennessee. She and her friend decided to call a truce and settled their long-standing, competitive feud by means of plea bargaining. She would be Number One in track, and her girl friend would be Number One in basketball.

At 14, as a high school student, she joined the Tiger-belles' track team and went into serious training at Tennessee State University after school and on weekends. On the campus she met a lovely young woman named Mae Faggs, who already had made two U.S. Olympic teams in the past. Mae was the only person—outside of Wilma's immediate family—with whom the teenager would share her dream. She also shared her frustrations of the early years, her ordeal with leg braces and how it felt having no opportunity to belong. The encouraging, nurturing, and training continued and so did her victories. By the end of the first summer, she had won the 75- and 100-yard dashes and was on the winning 440-yard relay team in the junior division at the national AAU meet in Philadelphia.

One day, nearly two years later, Mae Faggs came up to her and said to her protégée, "Would you like to make our Olympic team?" Her answer was typical of her youth, and reflected the fantasies of her many bus rides back and forth to Nashville: "Do we get to travel?"

"Yes, of course," Mae answered, "the 1956 Olympic Games are going to be in Australia."

"When do we leave?" she implored.

First they had to qualify at the Olympic trials at American University in Washington, D.C. During the 200-meter dash qualifying heats, she started out leading the pack. Finding herself out in front, ahead of Mae Faggs, she looked around to see where her friend was. Mae sped by and came in first. She came in second. "I'm disappointed in you," Mae scolded after the meet. "Qualifying isn't enough; you've got to always go for that gold."

Wilma was eliminated in the semifinals of the 200-meter dash at the 1956 Olympic Games in Melbourne, but went on to win a bronze medal as a member of the team finishing third in the women's 400-meter relay. She was part happy, part heartbroken during the remainder of her stay in Australia. She told herself that this kind of a performance wouldn't happen again; that next time, she would get it right. She was only 16, still in high school, and already committing herself to win in 1960!

Back home she resisted any temptation to take advantage of her new celebrity status. She could have thumbed her nose at the neighborhood kids who had been so cruel to her when she had been an invalid in those metal braces. Instead, she let them look at the bronze medal and talked with them about the thrill it had been to win it. Her former tormenters now were her friends as they relished that world class feeling that comes only once in a lifetime for a little town like Clarksville, Tennessee.

When we speak of dedication and persistence, there is a tendency to remember only the highlights and gloss over the agonizing realities of what it takes to be a "world class anything." It's important to remember that there were no athletic scholarships for women in those days, and that Wilma was paying her way as she attended Tennessee State University. At the same time, track workouts were going on every day. What's more, it was mandatory for each young woman to maintain a "B" average or better, and carry eighteen units in order to remain a member of the Tigerbelles track club.

To give herself the "winner's edge," she resorted to a type of extracurricular, do-it-yourself program, similar to what she had used years earlier when she was learning to walk without leg braces. When she realized that she was slipping behind the other girls on the team because of her work and study load, she began sneaking down the dormitory fire escape to run on the track from 8:00 to 10:00 P.M. Then she would climb back up the fire escape and into bed in time for "Lights Out" and "Bed Check." At sunrise, the grueling training schedule resumed. Every morning she would run at six o'clock and at ten o'clock, and in the afternoon again at three o'clock. Week after week, year after year, she maintained the same monotonous, demanding schedule. And this went on for over twelve hundred days!

A Living Legend

When Wilma walked out on the stadium field in the summer of 1960 in Rome, she was ready. The nearly 80,000 fans began to cheer wildly, sensing that she was to be one of those special Olympians who have captured the hearts of the spectators of the world throughout history (as Jesse Owens and Babe Didrikson did before her, and as Olga Korbut and Bruce Jenner would after her). As she began to warm up for the first event, the cadenced chant began to well up from the stands: "Vilma, Vilma, Vilma." There was never a doubt in her mind, or in theirs, who was to be standing on the top platform when the award presentations were made.

She turned in three electrifying performances by breezing to easy victories in the 100-meter and 200-meter dashes, and anchoring the U.S. women's team to a first place finish in the 400-meter relay. Three gold medals—the first woman in history ever to win three gold medals in track and field! And each of the three races was won in world record time.

She had been a little crippled girl who rode the bus to Nashville—isolated from her neighborhood but supported by her parents, family, and a few loyal friends. Now she was Wilma Rudolph, a living legend.

Since those moments in the stadium in Rome, much has happened to reward her for her discipline and sacrifices. There have been ticker tape parades, a private audience with President John F. Kennedy at the White House, the Female Athlete of the Year Award, and the prestigious Sullivan Award, presented to the top amateur athlete in the nation. (Wilma was the third woman in history to receive it.) Then followed a book, telling her life story, and the TV movie adaptation, *Wilma*, starring Cicely Tyson and Shirley Jo Finney. Through it all, the quiet dignity has remained intact. In response to her "living legend" accolades, Wilma answers frankly, "When you're running, you're involved; you're always in the process of trying to master something. And you never quite get there. I guess that's what makes the so-called champion; the willingness to continue to work and strive to improve your excellence every day."

I first met Wilma Rudolph in March of 1980 at an inspirational public rally in Olympia, Washington, sponsored by a local church group. Wilma, Norman Vincent Peale, and I were the featured speakers in a big gymnasium filled with several thousand children and adults. As Wilma began to tell her story, there was none of the gesturing, pontificating, or embellishing usually associated with platform personalities. The audience was in her hands, but she didn't put them there. They put themselves in her hands, because the story she told was real. It was not so much about the ecstasy of winning; it was more about the family, good friends, the problems, the prayers, the disappointments, and the struggle.

As she was nearing her closing remarks, Dr. Peale leaned over and whispered to me, "She's really some kind of human being, isn't she!" I nodded my agreement as I listened to her last words: "There may be world class athletes, and superstars, but that doesn't set them apart as world class people. I've had many of the same problems growing up as you have, and I hope my story in some small way can help one person believe that he or she can change, improve, and grow."

Today, you'll find Wilma giving a keynote address at a major convention, or helping some future Olympic star. What she loves best is giving classes, seminars, and financial support through the Wilma Rudolph Foundation in Indianapolis, helping someone get ahead, who is coming from behind.[1]

What Vince Lombardi Really Said

Wilma Rudolph turned out to be a winner against incredible odds. She would never let herself be defeated. She set her mind on winning and she did it. There seems to be a lot more to winning than being talented, having the best equipment, or the most financial resources.

Vince Lombardi, the legendary coach of the Green Bay Packers, has been labeled (falsely, in my opinion) as the "winning by intimidation" specialist. In many of the positive-thinking type films, his immortal slogan is pronounced: "Winning isn't everything; it's the *only* thing!"

I am not convinced Lombardi really said that, and if he did, I'm not certain that he is being interpreted correctly. A friend of mine from Wisconsin who heard Vince speak many times, and who is a Packer fan to the very chill of his bones, showed me some transcripts of Vince's talks. We looked at these transcripts of the charismatic mentor of the seemingly invincible Packer teams, and they read as follows:

"Winning isn't everything . . . but the *will* to win is everything."

The wording makes quite a difference, doesn't it? It is the will or the "faith in action" that makes the difference. Perhaps the most quoted and popular of all of

---

1. For more complete information on Wilma Rudolph see *Wilma: The Story of Wilma Rudolph*, Signet Books.

Vince Lombardi's homilies is one that has come to be the favorite of many leaders in every field.

The Secret behind Those Golden Arches

One afternoon my wife and I were invited to the home of Ray Kroc, founder of the world-famed McDonald's hamburger chain. Although we chatted for only thirty minutes or so, I learned a lot about the man behind McDonald's. Two slogans of his say more than pages of history could.

The first saying is one my grandmother used to repeat while we were working in her garden: "As long as you're green, you're growing; as soon as you're ripe, you start to rot."

Kroc's second saying is my favorite, and it was also Lombardi's favorite:

> Press On: Nothing in the world can take the place of persistence. Talent will not; nothing is more common than unsuccessful individuals with talent. Genius will not; unrewarded genius is almost a proverb. Education will not; the world is full of educated derelicts. Persistence and determination alone are omnipotent.[2]

That sums up why I believe perseverance is such an important best-kept secret of success. Everyone wants success, but few are willing to make the effort, to pay the price, and do what's required. In my teen seminars, I give each of the attendees a poem that I wrote—in poster form—that says basically the same thing as Lombardi's favorite homily. I think you'll enjoy having it as well:

---

2. Kroc, Ray A., *Grinding It Out* (New York: Berkley, 1978), p. 201.

If You Think You Can, You Can

You can be a total winner, even if you're a
    beginner,
  If you think you can, you can—if you
    think you can, you can;
You can wear the gold medallion, you can
    ride your own black stallion,
  If you think you can, you can—if you
    think you can, you can.
It's not your talent, or the gifted birth,
  It's not your bank book that determines
    worth;
And it isn't in the color of your skin,
  It's your attitude that lets you win!
You can upset McEnroe or Austin, win the
    marathon in Boston,
  If you think you can, you can—if you
    think you can, you can;
You can profit through inflation, you can
    redirect this nation,
  If you think you can, you can—if you
    think you can, you can.
It doesn't matter if you've won before,
  It makes no difference what the half-time
    score;
It's never over 'til the final gun,
  So keep on trying and you'll find you've
    won.
Just grab your dream and then believe it,
  Go out and work, and you'll achieve it;
If you think you can, you can—if you think
    you can, you can!
  Believe in God—and you're halfway
    there.
Believe in yourself—and you're
    three-quarters there.

Thinking that you can is only the first step. It takes weeks, months, and years of persistence to overcome the odds.

It's Never Too Late to Try

Ray Kroc, of McDonald's, is a classic example of an individual who never gave up on his dream. He really didn't hit his stride until he was 52. He began selling paper cups and playing the piano part-time to support his family in the early 1920s. After seventeen years with Lily Tulip Cup Company he became one of the company's top salesmen. But he gave up security with the company and struck out on his own in the milk shake machine business. He was impressed with a machine that could mix a number of milk shakes at the same time.

When he heard that the McDonald brothers were turning out forty milk shakes at one time on eight of his six-spindled Multimixer machines, he went out to San Bernardino to investigate. After observing the quality assembly-line production of burgers, french fries, and milk shakes, he could not conceive of that being wasted on just one location.

He asked the McDonald brothers, "Why don't you open other restaurants like this?"

They objected, saying, "it would be a lot of trouble," and that they "didn't know who they'd get to open them." Ray Kroc had just such a person in mind. That person was Ray Kroc.

The most important message in the McDonald's story, I think, is that although Ray Kroc paid his dues as a salesman and didn't begin his new business until he was 52, he was able to build McDonald's into a billion dollar business in twenty-two years! It took IBM forty-six years to reach one billion dollars in revenues, and Xerox sixty-three years.

Perseverance does not always mean sticking to the

same thing forever. It means giving full concentration and effort to whatever you are doing, right now! It means doing the tough things first and looking downstream for gratification and rewards. It means being happy in your work, but hungry for more knowledge and progress. It means making more calls, going more miles, pulling more weeds, getting up earlier in the day and always being on the lookout for a better way of doing what you're doing. Perseverance is success through trial and error.

The excitement is in knowing that most individuals don't really reach their prime productivity until much later in life than is usually thought. For young people, that means that there iş time to gain knowledge and develop a track record. For us older warriors, it means that there's still hope! If a paper cup salesman and piano player can build the biggest food service chain in the world and if a little girl from Tennessee can take off her leg braces and sprint to three gold medals as the fastest woman in the world, then, certainly, you can still make your dreams come true. The secret is perseverance. Press on! Never give up your dream!

Ten Action Steps toward Perseverance

1. Do high priority work first. The reason most people spend their time on low priority "busy work" is that it is easier to do and does not require additional knowledge, skills, or coordination with someone else. Set your priorities on a must-do-now, should-do-soon, and would-like-to-do-when-possible basis. Set them every day, no later than the early morning of the day you are beginning—preferably, the last action of the previous day.

2. Concentrate your time and energies on the 20 percent of your activities, contacts, and concepts that have proven most productive to you in the past. Remember the "80/20 rule" named after Vilfredo

Pareto, a nineteenth-century Italian economist: 80 percent of the production volume usually comes from 20 percent of the producers; and 80 percent of the product line. What this means is that you need to focus your sphere of influence on the most productive people and ideas.

3. Whenever you make a change in your life, from the current way you are doing something, anticipate a temporary drop in productivity and efficiency. Don't worry if a change you made in profession or life-style isn't bearing fruit right away. It takes time for change to be assimilated. As familiarity and confidence rebuild, the productivity will increase again. Don't stew; let it simmer a while.

4. If you fail the first time, try again. If you fail a second time, get more feedback as to why you failed. If you fail a third time, your sights might be too high for now. Bring your goals in just a little from the horizon.

5. Try to associate regularly with individuals having similar goals. Most individuals join a group with the same problems, i.e., overweight, smokers, etc. But I'm not talking about that. I'm talking about a group with the same values and dreams, not the same problems and habits. Getting together once a month can provide action ideas that really pay off. The group support also helps the perseverance.

6. If you are stymied or at a dead end with a problem, change your scenery and mood. You might try relaxing and reflecting by getting away for a day at the ocean or in the country. Remember that the right-brain creative problem solver in your mind is always available for review, when your left-brain logic slows down. This is not escaping or stewing. It is landscaping and renewing.

7. Always expect the unexpected.

8. After you have gained general knowledge in a field or subject, concentrate on learning one aspect of it well. Succeed in specializing, before you diversify. Doing one thing well, until you have mastered it, brings confidence and a reputation for excellence. Jack Nicklaus has mastered playing the game of golf. Now he can do what he has always wanted to do—design golf courses!

9. Be honest and logical when you approach your problems. Generally there are only two types of problems: those that are easy to solve (actually these are really only projects that people want to deal with), and those that have reached an emergency state and are "urgent." A good way to measure your problems is to ask yourself: "Am I spending my time on what's important to me and my family, or am I always under the gun meeting deadlines?"

10. Do more than you are asked and contribute more than is required. Go the extra mile. Remember, winners see rainbows in thunderstorms—and ice skates instead of icy streets. Live out the story of the little boy who bought a new pair of ice skates with his allowance so he could skate on the frozen pond. His mother, watching him slide, slip, and fall every time he tried to stand up, ran to his rescue, cautioning: "Let's put them away, before you get hurt!" The boy continued struggling: "Mom, I didn't get them to give up with—I got my skates to learn with!"

Questions about Your Perseverance

1. Do you complete what you start? Always? Usually? Eventually?

2. Are you discouraged easily? What do you do to fight back?

waterfront. The opera house is truly unique; but there is much more upon which to feast your eyes and mind.

Sydney is like San Diego and San Francisco combined, with a life-style that is, surprisingly, faster paced than either of the two. The harbor stretches out as far as the eye can see, and is alive with every imaginable type of seagoing vehicle. Ferryboats, tugboats, outboards, inboards, hydrofoils, Hovercraft, Navy ships, excursion boats, trawlers, freighters, liners, cruisers, yachts, and sailboats all seem to be part of one giant regatta—with the trial races run during the week and the free-for-all finals held every weekend. I have never seen so many sailboats. Sydney harbor on Sunday makes Newport harbor look like a children's bathtub.

My wife and I have been traveling "down under" to Australia twice each year for the past five years. We love the magnificent abundance of the open terrain there. It offers a nostalgic look back into America's rugged, pioneering past. It also holds a rich promise of mineral resources and technological advancement which is unmatched almost anywhere else in the world. We love the warmth and humor of the "Aussies." On our first visit, during our taxi ride to the Wentworth Hotel from the airport, I initiated a friendly conversation with our driver, who was a man in his late sixties or early seventies.

"Absolutely beautiful morning today, isn't it?" I offered happily, eyeing his face through the rearview mirror. He said nothing for a moment and then pulled the cab over and stopped beside the road. He proceeded to get out of the cab, turn around in a circle, taking deep breaths, stretching, and looking up in the sky. I wondered if he were having a seizure.

When he got back in the taxi, he winked at me and grinned: "You're sure right on, Mate. It is a lovely day. I've been driving since midnight and I hadn't been out in it yet to notice the conditions. But it's a real beaut' all right." My wife and I chuckled all the way into the city. Before we arrived at the hotel, I asked the driver to take us on a tour of Sydney.

"What would you like to see and where would you most like to go?" he said, cocking his head to one side.

"We really don't care at all," my wife and I chimed in together, "take us anyplace you want to go."

He took us to his home for breakfast. He said he was a bit hungry and introduced us to Vegemite on toast and a cup of "white" coffee.

On our latest trip, we took the Ansett airbus shuttle from Sydney to Brisbane for our final week of lectures and seminars, before a brief vacation at one of the Great Barrier Reef islands. After the Great Barrier Reef we were scheduled to make a three-day speaking swing through New Zealand and then set sail for California, via Honolulu. On the shuttle flight, as I gazed down at the red-tiled roofs and inland estuaries that seem to go on forever, the pilot banked the plane slightly to a northeast heading toward Queensland. I wondered—suddenly—why I was always on an airplane.

Running to or Running from?

Since my "Psychology of Winning" cassette album hit the best-sellers' list in 1978, I have been on the road virtually every weekday. Have you ever heard of anyone who climbed aboard an airplane nearly every day for five consecutive years? Even airline pilots don't fly that much! It had become so bad that my dog hid behind the gardener and growled at me when I came home, and I preferred plastic silverware to eat my dinner with. I haven't checked the *Guinness Book of Records*, but I'll wager I would be in the running.

That is the word I was searching for—*running!* Was I running to or running from my fulfillment? I reclined my seat-back and politely declined the tea and cakes offered by the stewardess.

As I began to ponder the question, I glanced over at

Susan, who has managed to join me on a majority of my business trips. She was reading *The Thornbirds* and didn't notice me watching her. Studying her face, I marveled at her ability to nourish our six children, manage an immaculate home, and still be able to support me lovingly and beautifully on this whirlwind lecture schedule. I bless the day we met. To remind each other of the joy of our relationship, Susan and I celebrate two anniversaries each year. Every October 30, we celebrate our first encounter. We try to recreate that initial stroll on the beach near Sarasota, Florida, where we took a picnic lunch and got sandspurs in the cuffs of our jeans. Our wedding anniversary is on the 5th of May. We like to be alone on that day, preferably at home.

As the pilot lowered the landing gear for our descent into Brisbane, I thought about how far from home we were. I thought about the children and reflected back on my own childhood fantasies. Ever since I can remember I have dreamed of international travel and following the sun to Australia. I had read books, studied atlases and sat in on slide presentations. Every time I saw a Qantas commercial on television, I thought of Sydney, Perth, Adelaide, Melbourne, and Brisbane. When the children would giggle with glee and point out the cute little koala bear sitting on the raft in the ocean at the end of the Qantas commercial, I would remind them koalas were really not bears at all—they were marsupials. I would show the kids where Australia was on the map and promise them I'd take them all there . . . someday.

As we taxied to the ramp to disembark, I thought of how quickly that "someday" had become "yesterday" and two years ago. We have travelled throughout the United States, Canada, Mexico, Central America, the Caribbean, and Europe. The children have travelled extensively with us, partly because we wanted to broaden their understanding of different cultures and mostly because we love to be around them.

During the limousine ride to Brisbane's Parkroyal Hotel, I still was hounded by the questions that had flashed into my mind shortly after takeoff from Sydney. *Why am I always on airplanes? Am I running to or from my fulfillment? What's it all about, Alfie?* I dismissed the silly questions and got my slide carousel tray out of the trunk to complete the audiovisual setup for the afternoon and evening seminar, following the press conference.

The gnawing questions returned shortly after I began my "Psychology of Winning" lecture to the one thousand executives and their spouses in the Parkroyal ballroom. I always start my programs by reciting my own version of Edgar A. Guest's poem, "Sermons We See." I have changed it to apply to "winning" as being the example we set for others:

I'd Rather Watch a Winner

I'd rather watch a winner, than hear one any
    day,
I'd rather have one walk with me than
    merely show the way.
The eye's a better pupil and more willing
    than the ear;
Fine counsel is confusing, but example's
    always clear.
And the best of all the coaches are the ones
    who live their creeds;
For to see the good in action is what
    everybody needs.
I can soon learn how to do it if you'll let me
    see it done;
I can watch your hands in action, but your
    tongue too fast may run.
And the lectures you deliver may be very
    wise and true;
But I'd rather get my lessons by observing
    what you do.

> For I may misunderstand you and the high
> advice you give;
> But there's no misunderstanding how you
> act and how you live.
> I'd rather watch a winner, than hear one any
> day!

As I began to cover the goal-setting exercises after the break about 9:00 P.M., I really found myself doing some deep soul-searching. I was giving the lecture, but it was as if I were a bystander watching myself going through the motions. There was one of those reminder phrases again: "going through the motions." *Is that what I am doing?* I wondered. *Am I trying to help these individuals grow in their lives or am I trying to prove something to myself? What has been my obsession in travelling constantly for the past four years? Why have I not devoted more hours to being a model for my own children? Why do I always talk about quality of time, instead of quantity of time with them?*

I focused in again on the workshop as we moved toward the last section on self-dimension and perspective. During the goal-setting session they had completed their "Wheel of Fortune" goal sheets and discussed the results in small mastermind groups. The seminar was going well. Apparently, the registrants had not noticed my preoccupation with my own conscience during the first half of the program.

I passed out the second set of "Wheel of Fortune" illustrations. Throughout the world, teenagers, executives, and couples have found the self-dimension exercise one of their more meaningful experiences.

"Please turn to the page entitled *Self-Dimension Grid*. On this grid there are 24 different items. You will notice the numbers across the top of the page range from 10 points to 100 points. Reading each of the 24 separate items, ask yourself the question, 'How true is this of me?'—in other words, taking the first item, 'Have a variety of close friends,' is this 10 percent true of you, 20, 30, 60, 80, or 100 percent true of you? Rate yourself on each item, circling the dot under the percentage point at which you see yourself. It should only take you about 8 to 10 minutes to complete this grid."

Self-Dimension Grid

	10	20	30	40	50	60	70	80	90	100
1. Have a variety of close friends.	.	.	.	.	.	.	.	.	.	.
2. Spend time alone thinking, meditating, or praying often.	.	.	.	.	.	.	.	.	.	.
3. Exercise vigorously each day.	.	.	.	.	.	.	.	.	.	.
4. Have adequate quality and quantity time spent with family.	.	.	.	.	.	.	.	.	.	.
5. Have a job that pays me well.	.	.	.	.	.	.	.	.	.	.
6. Am already engaged in the career I want.	.	.	.	.	.	.	.	.	.	.
7. Am involved in community activities.	.	.	.	.	.	.	.	.	.	.
8. Enjoy reading nonfiction books.	.	.	.	.	.	.	.	.	.	.
9. Make friends easily.	.	.	.	.	.	.	.	.	.	.
10. Have studied Bible or religious history.	.	.	.	.	.	.	.	.	.	.
11. Eat nutritious, well-balanced meals.	.	.	.	.	.	.	.	.	.	.
12. Regularly write or call members of the family.	.	.	.	.	.	.	.	.	.	.
13. Am creating an adequate retirement fund.	.	.	.	.	.	.	.	.	.	.
14. See unusual opportunities for advancement in my career.	.	.	.	.	.	.	.	.	.	.
15. Belong to local association(s) within the community.	.	.	.	.	.	.	.	.	.	.
16. Enjoy educational TV programs.	.	.	.	.	.	.	.	.	.	.

	10	20	30	40	50	60	70	80	90	100
17. Enjoy meeting new people and going to parties or group events.	.		.		.	.		.	.	.
18. Attend church, synagogue, or religious services.	.	.	.	.	.	.	.			
19. Am involved in sports regularly.	.	.	.	.	.	.	.	.		
20. Enjoy family reunions/gatherings.	.	.	.	.	.	.	.			
21. Have a substantial savings account.	.	.	.	.	.	.	.	.		
22. Am really good at and enjoy my work.		.	.	.	.	.	.			
23. Have volunteered for a community project.	.	.	.	.	.	.	.	.		
24. Like to go to museums, fairs, libraries to see what's new.	.	.	.	.	.	.	.	.	.	

"Now please turn to the next sheet called *Balanced Living*. In the self-dimension grid you just completed, you were asked to rate yourself in the areas of your life. For example, numbers 1, 9, and 17 relate to your social life. Numbers 3, 11, and 19 cover the physical area of your life, etc. Transfer each of the percentage scores for each of the 24 items from the self-dimension grid page to the balanced living page. Add the numbers in each of the eight columns and total them up."

Balanced Living

"Add the numbers on your grid for the following areas of your life:

SOCIAL	SPIRITUAL	PHYSICAL	FAMILY
1. _____	2. _____	3. _____	4. _____
9. _____	10. _____	11. _____	12. _____
17. _____	18. _____	19. _____	20. _____
TOTAL	TOTAL	TOTAL	TOTAL

		COMMUNITY	
FINANCIAL	PROFESSIONAL	SUPPORT	MENTAL
5. _____	6. _____	7. _____	8. _____
13. _____	14. _____	15. _____	16. _____
21. _____	22. _____	23. _____	24. _____
_____	_____	_____	_____
TOTAL	TOTAL	TOTAL	TOTAL

"Now turn to the 'Wheel of Fortune' and plot the total points for each of the eight areas of your life on the line below the title of the area. When you have plotted all eight points, connect them to get dimension or perspective on the shape and size of your own wheel. How round is your wheel? How will it roll down the road of life? Which areas of your life would you like to spend more time developing? For example,

THE WHEEL OF FORTUNE

is there too much emphasis on profession and finance, and not enough on physical or family?"

I was asking these questions of my audience, but they were echoing in my own ears. They were not questions being asked by me. Suddenly, they were questions I was asking of me!

Living on "Someday I'll"

My wife noticed that I seemed a little subdued as I drew the meeting to a conclusion at 10:30 P.M. I closed with my own verse on perspective in life, which points out the importance of not being a bystander in life. It has more significance for me than any of my other poetry:

> There is an Island fantasy
> A "Someday I'll," we'll never see
> When recession stops, inflation ceases
> Our mortgage is paid, our pay increases
> That Someday I'll where problems end
> Where every piece of mail is from a friend
> Where the children are sweet and already
>   grown
> Where all the other nations can go it alone
> Where we all retire at forty-one
> Playing backgammon in the island sun
> Most unhappy people look to tomorrow
> To erase this day's hardship and sorrow
> They put happiness on "lay away"
> And struggle through a blue today
> But happiness cannot be sought
> It can't be earned, it can't be bought
> Life's most important revelation
> Is that the journey means more than the
>   destination
> Happiness is where you are right now
> Pushing a pencil or pushing a plow
> Going to school or standing in line
> Watching and waiting, or tasting the wine
> If you live in the past you become senile
> If you live in the future you're on Someday
>   I'll
> The fear of results is procrastination
> The joy of today is a celebration
> You can save, you can slave, trudging mile
>   after mile

But you'll never set foot on your Someday
    I'll
When you've paid all your dues and put in
    your time
Out of nowhere comes another Mt. Everest
    to climb
From this day forward make it your vow
Take Someday I'll and make it your Now!

After the last seminar participant had left the ballroom, Susan and I walked slowly to the lobby and took the "lift" up to our room. "You seem a little distant and sad," she said. "Is everything all right . . . weren't you pleased with the program?"

I poured a glass of lemon squash for each of us and sighed: "I was pleased with the audience's response. I am more concerned about the meaning of my words on the stranger who was giving the program!"

She looked puzzled. "What do you mean, *stranger?*" She searched my eyes.

"That was a stranger who gave that program tonight," I whispered painfully, looking out the window at the deserted park. "The real Denis Waitley is home working in our rose garden, with his wife playing with his kids and dog. That guy standing up there was living on 'Someday I'll'!"

We went to bed, quietly, holding each other closely. The next morning we left for a couple of days of relaxation on Heron Island near the Great Barrier Reef.

The Riddle of the Reef

When we arrived on the island, I was determined to do a little fishing. The only boat available was a ten-foot aluminum rowboat. I took it anyway because I wanted to get out beyond that reef line for some peace of mind and communion with my Creator. Although I was used to cabin cruisers, with live-bait tanks and flying bridges, my little rowboat and drop line would have to do today. The swells and surf were rougher than I had anticipated, but having been born and raised in La Jolla, I was unconcerned. I rowed out farther than I should have and soon I was out of sight of the rocky cove where Susan was sunbathing. I put a piece of squid on my hook and lowered my line about thirty feet to the bottom, having not the slightest notion what was down there.

To this day, I still don't know the exact sequence of events during that next sixty seconds. The fish must have weighed at least twenty pounds by the force of the tug on my drop line. It was pulling my arms out over the stern of the boat, and I must have tried to stand up to gain some leverage. The boat capsized. In the next instant I was in the water, with the anchor line wrapped around my leg and sinking with the aluminum boat. The adrenaline began to flow and my heart rate soared as instant reality hit me. This was not a seminar or one of my simulation drills. This was not a Peter Benchley fiction adventure, with a Denis Waitley look-alike. I was in immediate danger of losing more than the fish and the boat.

Having been a carrier-based attack pilot trained in survival, and a strong swimmer, I did not panic. I was the coolest, middle-aged, completely out-of-shape, ex-pilot in the ocean. It took me well over a minute to untangle myself from the anchor line and struggle to the surface. Gasping for breath, it took only another minute to survey the situation. I was eight thousand miles from my home, off the Great Barrier Reef of Australia. There were no other boats, and I was more than a mile offshore. No one could hear me or see me and I already was winded from being underwater so long.

I had told my wife I would be back by 2:00 P.M., which gave me another three hours in which to drown comfortably before she would begin to become concerned. I was fairly certain that I could not swim the distance to shore, without being pulled by the strong current into the huge breakers that were crashing into the reef at the mouth of the cove. My only hope for survival was to salvage the boat. I still had the anchor chain in my hand and, operating on the principle that objects weigh less underwater than out of it, I started slowly pulling my ten-foot "last hope" toward the surface.

It took at least another hour to inch the boat up close to the surface by pulling on the anchor line. By that time the current had swept me dangerously close to the first group of coral formations approaching the reef. I decided to let the breakers carry me on to the coral so that I could try to land upright on top of one of the rocks and simultaneously right the small aluminum boat. Looking back at the odds, it was the most ridiculous gamble I could have considered. I must admit, however, I was putting a lot of faith in the Lord to slow down the interval of the waves and help me stand up the first time through.

The first big wave threw me over the rocks into the swirling eddy currents. The boat was dented but still intact. I let the rip current pull me away from the rocks and positioned myself, with the submerged boat, for the next set. Somehow the next wave knocked me on and off the rocks and flipped the rowboat upside down, emptying the water that had kept it submerged. I managed to right the boat, and paddled it, half full of seawater, away from the rocks and toward the cove a mile away.

Although I was numb and exhausted, I was elated with the prospect that God had seen fit to let me live one more day. When I looked down at my legs, I wasn't so sure. My legs had been gashed on the coral and I was trailing blood behind the boat. My heart jumped up in my throat as I thought of "Quint" chumming for the great white shark in the movie *Jaws*. Have you ever seen a dented, ten-foot rowboat, with no oars, travel a mile in under half an hour?

Sitting by the cove with bandaged shins the following day, it was appropriate that I had selected *The Star Thrower,* by the late Loren Eiseley, to read and recuperate with. I hadn't told my wife how close she had come to being "insurance rich." I didn't want to concern her and, besides, why should I share my own stupidity with someone who still believed I was brilliant? I thumbed through the book until I found the title selection in Eiseley's banquet of essays. After I finished reading the fourteen-page essay, I closed the book and laid it down on the blanket. I took Susan by the hand and we went for a walk by the tidal pools, stepping very slowly and carefully among the rocks due to the stiffness in my legs. I had discovered, by serendipity, the tenth best-kept secret of total success.

Celebrating Instead of Collecting

When Eiseley wrote *The Star Thrower* he must have had someone like me in mind. It is the story of a man, my age, who goes to the seashore to try to gain perspective on the meaning of life. It reminds me very much of one of my favorite books, *Gift from the Sea,* by Anne Morrow Lindbergh. From the moment I read the story, and considered its meaning, I decided that I have been placed upon the earth to be a Star Thrower. It is interesting that I, as a Christian, can interpret an essay written by a humanist and naturalist, finding profound spiritual significance in it for me. This is one of God's great gifts—his disciples can learn from every experience.

The Star Thrower tells of a man, in his prime, who observes the shell collectors at the beach in the height of tourist season, particularly after a storm, engaged in a kind of greedy madness to outcollect their less aggressive neighbors. He watches them scrambling along the beach at dawn with bundles of gathered starfish, hermit crabs, sea urchins, and other living shells. Arguing, toppling over each other, overburdened, they rush in a kind of frenzy to outdo each other for these fine specimens. The shell collectors then boil the shell "houses," occupants included, in outdoor kettles provided by the resort hotels as a service to guests who will show off their proud collections to envious relatives and friends back home.

I have met many people with the collectors' morality. They are not unique to the seashore. They are in every country, every city, and every home. They are the people who are trying to collect life and own happiness. They are the consumers.

As I became engrossed in Eiseley's book, I thought how easily I could have been the middle-aged man in the story.

The man noticed a solitary human figure standing near the water's edge in the center of a rainbow caused by the sun-filled spray. The figure stooped over, then stood up to fling an object out to sea beyond the breaking surf. The spectator (who could have been me) finally reached the older figure and asked him what he was doing. The old man with the bronzed, worn face answered softly, "I'm a star thrower."

Expecting to see a sand dollar, or perhaps a flat rock—like the ones he used to sail across the water for fun—the younger man came closer for a better look. The old man, with a quick yet gentle movement, picked up another starfish and spun it gracefully far out into the sea. "It may live," he said, "if the offshore pull is strong enough."

Here was a human being who was not a collector. He said he had decided to be part of life and had dedicated himself to helping give another day, another week, another year, another opportunity for living. The younger man, silently, reached down and skipped a still-living star across the water toward freedom. He felt like a gardener sowing—sowing the seeds of life. He looked back over his shoulder. Against the rainbow, the old Star Thrower stooped and flung once more. He understood the secret.

The Secret Within

The Star Thrower's secret is for all of us to know—and live by. Life cannot be collected. Happiness cannot be travelled to, owned, earned, worn, or consumed. Happiness is the spiritual experience of living every minute with love, grace, and gratitude. The gift of life is not a treasure hunt. You cannot look for success. The treasure is within you. It only needs to be uncovered and discovered. The secret is to turn a life of collection into a life of celebration.

All the best-kept secrets of success involve your perspective—how you see life from within. The Seeds of Greatness are the responses or attitudes you develop as a result of "seeing" the world more clearly. When you see more clearly, you see yourself as valuable and your self-esteem grows strong. Seeing clearly enables your imagination to create and soar. Seeing more clearly gives you the understanding that you are responsible for learning as much and contributing as much as you can to life.

When you see life from within, you see wisdom, purpose, and faith as cornerstones of your family's foundation. You see through the eyes of love and reach out and touch all those with whom you come in contact. Seeing from within is having the courage to adapt to change and to persevere when the odds seem overwhelming. Seeing from within is believing that beauty and goodness are worth planting every day.

In this chapter I have not called attention to the best-kept secret in the way I have all the others. That is because perspective—seeing life from within—is not only the tenth and final secret; it is the very essence of all that I have written in this book. How we see life makes all the difference.

My grandmother had planted the seeds in me as we worked in her garden, by teaching me how to "see" life. Many people go through their lives stepping on the flowers, while pointing out the weeds. Grandma taught me how to pull out the weeds, while reveling in and savoring the splendor and the fragrance of the flowers.

I Know You Understand

I'll always remember the Christmas Eve I got that call. I was in Florida completing some research foundation work, before returning to California. It was our first Christmas away from our parents and grandparents. I heard my mother's voice whispering softly at the other end of the line. She was telling me about my grandma, the unforgettable lady who had planted those Seeds of Greatness in me so many years before.

My grandmother had been up and dressed as usual by six in the morning. She had packed a few incidentals in a small overnight bag and was sitting on her bed when my mother came in her room. At the hospital, they took the standard tests for an 87-year-old, when she's feeling weak. They decided to admit her and run some tests. She had never been in a hospital and asked if she might go home and come back some other time, when it was more convenient for everyone.

She wanted to be home with the family on Christmas, as had been her tradition for over eight decades. The doctor insisted that she stay and she quietly conceded. She brushed her hair and dressed herself in a lovely pink housecoat, with a pretty bow tied at the neck. She and my mother chatted about the menu for the family dinner to be held the following night.

It was nearly sunset, my mother said. Christmas music was playing softly at the nurses' station. My grandmother patted my mother on the hand and urged her to go home for a while. It had been a long day and there was still a lot for my mother to do to prepare for the Christmas gathering.

"You go on home. I'll be just fine," my grandma assured my mom, "I just want to have some time to myself and see this beautiful sunset."

Reluctantly, my mother had left, calling back her promise that she would return soon. In the next few minutes, Grandma had seen her last sunset—only to wake up and see her Lord face-to-face.

As I said good-bye to my mother and hung up the phone, my eyes filled with tears. I walked out of the door and went into the garden. I picked a flower and sat down on the earth. It was commencement day for my grandmother. Another beginning—another new garden for her. Faithfully she had tended the one on this earth. Now she had moved up to a more beautiful landscape.

As I thought of her, my memories returned to Grandma's garden where we used to sit and talk in the shade of her plumcot tree those many years ago. I could still hear her gentle words:

"You always get out what you put in, my child. Plant apple seeds and you get apple trees; plant the seeds of great ideas, and you will get great individuals. Do you understand what I mean?"

I understand now. I know you understand, too.

Denis Waitley has become one of the most sought after keynote speakers and seminar leaders in the nation for corporate, institutional, and public audiences. For more information on scheduling his live appearances, as well as video, film, and audio presentations on personal and professional excellence, please call or write:

Denis Waitley, Inc.
P. O. Box 197
Rancho Santa Fe, CA 92067
(619) 756-4201